THE MEANING OF "IN CHRIST"

IN THE GREEK NEW TESTAMENT

Clarence B. Hale

Summer Institute of Linguistics, Inc.

© 1991 by SIL International®
Library of Congress Catalog No: 2017961178
ISBN: 978-1-55671-440-5

Printed in the United States of America

No part of this publication may be reproduced, stored in a retrieval system, or transmitted in any form or by any means—electronic, mechanical, photocopy, recording, or otherwise—without the express permission of SIL International®. However, short passages, generally understood to be within the limits of fair use, may be quoted without written permission.

Copies of this and other publications of SIL International® may be obtained through distributors such as Amazon, Barnes & Noble, other worldwide distributors and, for select volumes, www.sil.org/resources/publications:

SIL International Publications
7500 W. Camp Wisdom Road
Dallas, Texas 75236-5629 USA

General inquiry: publications_intl@sil.org
Pending order inquiry: sales_intl@sil.org
www.sil.org/resources/publications

This book was produced from a digitally scanned reproduction of the original publication.

Cover Design
Barbara Alber

INTRODUCTION

Reason for the study

The phrase ἐν Χριστῷ 'in Christ' occurs 84 times in the Greek New Testament. Its equivalent expressions, ἐν Ἰησοῦ 'in Jesus', ἐν κυρίῳ 'in the Lord', ἐν τῷ υἱῷ 'in the Son', ἐν τῷ ἠγαπημένῳ 'in the beloved', ἐν τῷ ἐνδυναμοῦντι 'in the one strengthening', ἐν αὐτῷ (= ἐν Χριστῷ) 'in him', and ἐν ᾧ (= ἐν Χριστῷ) 'in whom', occur another 90 times. The minimum literal English translation for ἐν Χριστῷ 'in Christ' is usually found in the King James, the American Standard, the Revised Standard, and the New American Standard versions. This rendering, to be sure, has the advantage of being close to the form of the Greek original, but in many passages so brief a translation does not allow the context to make any contribution to the total meaning of the phrase. Consequently, the result is little more than a transliteration, such as we have in the English "I baptize" for the Greek βαπτίζω.

The preposition ἐν in other contexts is used with much variety of meaning. Bauer (BAGD) recognizes four main classifications: (1) local, (2) temporal, (3) causal, and (4) miscellaneous. A cursory examination of the way ἐν is treated, pp. 258–261, will quickly give an impression of the broad range of meanings possible for this little word. The presence of Χριστῷ 'Christ', of course, constitutes a considerable restraint. Even so, much more variety of application than I have found seems desirable in specific passages.

Apparently recognizing both the possible contributions of context and the limitation imposed by the minimum translation, J. B. Phillips, Kenneth Taylor, Charles B. Williams, and the committee responsible for the New English Bible have endeavored to vary the rendering of ἐν Χριστῷ 'in Christ' to suit different passages. These variations are to some extent instructive but for many passages the question still remains: "What does ἐν Χριστῷ 'in Christ' mean in the Greek New Testament?"

In the summer of 1972 at Ixmiquilpan, Mexico, John Beekman and Richard Blight encouraged me to investigate the possibility of finding a more satisfactory answer to this question than was then available. The results of my study were published in *Notes on Translation*, Number 52, June, 1974. Katy Barnwell and Richard Blight have proposed that several other prepositional phrases which are practically synonymous with ἐν Χριστῷ be included. It is hoped that this revision and expansion will prove helpful and that the suggested translations will be stimulating to translators.

Scope of the data

If my count is correct, ἐν Χριστῷ 'in Christ' and its equivalent expressions occur 174 times in the New Testament. In general, lexicons in their efforts to systematize the various possible meanings of ἐν fail to help in many particular contexts.

Although most frequently adverbial in its use, ἐν Χριστῷ 'in Christ' functions also as an adjective and as a substantive. Often the syntax may be explained in more than one way. I have found 51 possibilities of an adverbial construction, 57 of a substantival, and 31 of an adjectival.

Conclusions reached in this study

The translation of ἐν Χριστῷ 'in Christ' should vary with the syntax and the vocabulary of the context in which it stands. The following display of all the New Testament passages concerned will not solve all the problems connected with this short prepositional phrase, but it may suggest to a translator still other ways of expressing what seems to be the intended meaning of the writers.

DISPLAY OF PASSAGES USING ἐν Χριστῷ 'IN CHRIST' AND OTHER EQUIVALENT EXPRESSIONS

The phrase ἐν Χριστῷ 'in Christ' and its equivalent expressions, ἐν Ἰησοῦ 'in Jesus', ἐν κυρίῳ 'in the Lord', ἐν τῷ υἱῷ 'in the Son', ἐν τῷ ἠγαπημένῳ 'in the beloved', ἐν τῷ ἐνδυναμοῦντι 'in the one strengthening', ἐν αὐτῷ (= ἐν Χριστῷ) 'in him', and ἐν ᾧ (= ἐν Χριστῷ) 'in whom' are examined.

Enough Greek has been quoted to give some idea of the context of the portion for translations which are suggested. What is involved in the translation has in each instance been made bold. I have next described the syntax as I see it and then offered possible translations. Occasionally I have explained a translation which does not closely parallel the Greek.

Translations are mine unless credited to some other source. I have taken the liberty of inserting parentheses in any translation to try to show how much is contextual deduction. The following abbreviations are used for the sources mentioned with the suggested translations:

BAGD   Bauer, Walter. *A Greek-English Lexicon of the New Testament and Other Early Christian Literature*, translated and adapted from the 5th ed., 1958 by William F. Arndt and F. Wilbur Gingrich, 2d English ed. revised and augmented by F. Wilbur Gingrich and Frederick W. Danker. Chicago: University of Chicago Press, 1979.
CBW   C. B. Williams, *The New Testament: A Translation in the Language of the People*. Chicago: Moody Press, 1956.
JBP   J. B. Phillips, *The New Testament in Modern English*. New York: Macmillan, 1958.
LB   *The Living Bible*, Wheaton: Tyndale House, 1971.
NASB   *The New American Standard Bible*, Anaheim, Calif.: Foundation Press, 1973.
NEB   *The New English Bible*. Oxford and Cambridge: University Press, 1970.
NIV   *The Holy Bible, New International Version*. Grand Rapids: Zondervan Bible Publishers, 1978.
WFB   William F. Beck, *The New Testament in the Language of Today*. St. Louis: Concordia, 1963.

Acts 4:2
... διαπονούμενοι διὰ τὸ διδάσκειν αὐτοὺς τὸν λαὸν καὶ καταγγέλλειν ἐν τῷ Ἰησοῦ τὴν ἀνάστασιν τὴν ἐκ νεκρῶν ...

Syntax: ἐν τῷ Ἰησοῦ serves as an adverb modifying (1) only καταγγέλλειν 'to proclaim', or (2) both διδάσκειν 'to teach', and καταγγέλλειν, or (3) the verbal idea in ἀνάστασιν 'resurrection'.

Suggested translations:
For (1) "... because they were teaching the people and proclaiming the resurrection of the dead by (citing the example of) Jesus' (resurrection) ..."
For (2) "... because by (citing the example of) Jesus' (resurrection) they were teaching the people and proclaiming the resurrection of the dead ..."
For (3) "... because they were teaching the people and proclaiming the resurrection of the dead, (which would be brought about by the power of) Jesus ..."

Acts 4:10
... γνωστὸν ἔστω πᾶσιν ὑμῖν καὶ παντὶ τῷ λαῷ Ἰσραὴλ ὅτι ἐν τῷ ὀνόματι Ἰησοῦ Χριστοῦ τοῦ Ναζωραίου, ὃν ὑμεῖς ἐσταυρώσατε, ὃν ὁ θεὸς ἤγειρεν ἐκ νεκρῶν, ἐν τούτῳ οὗτος παρέστηκεν ἐνώπιον ὑμῶν ὑγιής.

Syntax: ἐν τούτῳ 'in this one' serves as an adverb modifying παρέστηκεν 'he stands'. τούτῳ is ambiguous in its grammatical gender. It may be considered (1) masculine with Ἰησοῦ Χριστοῦ 'Jesus Christ' as its antecedent, or (2) neuter with ὀνόματι 'name' as its antecedent. Since two relative clauses (ὃν ... ἐσταυρώσατε and ὃν ... νεκρῶν) intervene, and since the antecedent of each ὃν 'whom' is Ἰησοῦ Χριστοῦ, it may be that ἐν τούτῳ picks up ἐν τῷ ὀνόματι 'in the name'. On the other hand, τούτῳ may be expected to refer to the nearer of two possible antecedents.

Suggested translations:
For (1) "... this man stands before you in a sound physical condition (as the result of a miracle performed) by (Jesus)."
"... because of (Jesus)."
"... (healed) by (Jesus)."
For (2) "... because of it (i.e. Jesus' name) ..."
(NIV) "... It is by the name of Jesus Christ of Nazareth, whom you crucified but whom God raised from the dead, that this man stands before you healed."

Remark: The NIV translators may have decided that the repetition of the idea in the antecedent of τούτῳ was unnecessary. The omission of a translation of ἐν τούτῳ does not distort the meaning of the passage and may indicate that the NIV committee felt that ὀνόματι 'name' is the antecedent of τούτῳ.

Romans 3:24
... δικαιούμενοι δωρεὰν τῇ αὐτοῦ χάριτι διὰ **τῆς ἀπολυτρώσεως τῆς ἐν Χριστῷ Ἰησοῦ** ...

Syntax: ἐν Χριστῷ Ἰησοῦ is a prepositional phrase used as an adjective in restrictive attributive position to modify ἀπολυτρώσεως 'redemption'. We may supply οὔσης 'being' between τῆς and ἐν Χριστῷ. This construction is often faithfully rendered by an English relative clause. BAGD assigns a causal function for ἐν.

Suggested translations:
"... the redemption which (has been provided) by Christ Jesus ..."
"... the redemption which (is available through faith) in Christ Jesus ..."
"... the redemption which (has been accomplished) by Christ Jesus ..."
"... the redemption which (is a part of the privilege of being) in Christ Jesus ..."
(NASB) "... the redemption which (is) in Christ Jesus ..."
(NIV) "... the redemption that (came) by Christ Jesus ..."

Romans 6:11
οὕτως καὶ ὑμεῖς λογίζεσθε ἑαυτοὺς εἶναι νεκροὺς μὲν τῇ ἁμαρτίᾳ ζῶντας δὲ τῷ θεῷ ἐν Χριστῷ Ἰησοῦ.

Syntax: ἐν Χριστῷ Ἰησοῦ may be taken as an adverbial modifier (1) of εἶναι 'to be', (2) of ζῶντας 'living', or (3) of an ὄντι 'being' supplied to agree with θεῷ 'God'. This chapter has stated in vs. 5 the identity of the believer with Christ both in his death and in his resurrection. So ἐν Χριστῷ Ἰησοῦ is not limited to modifying ζῶντας 'living'. It has an adverbial function with εἶναι 'to be'. The believer is both dead to sin in Christ and alive to God in Christ.

Suggested translations:
For (1) "So you too consider yourselves (because you are identified) with Christ Jesus, to be dead to sin but alive to God."

(WFB) "So you too, (because you are) in Christ Jesus think of yourselves as dead to sin and living for God."
For (2) "So you too consider yourselves to be dead to sin, but, (because of what) Christ Jesus (has done), alive to God."
For (3) "So you too consider yourselves to be dead in relation to sin but alive in relation to God, (who is) in Christ Jesus."

Romans 6:23
τὰ γὰρ ὀψώνια τῆς ἁμαρτίας θάνατος, τὸ δὲ χάρισμα τοῦ θεοῦ ζωὴ αἰώνιος ἐν Χριστῷ Ἰησοῦ τῷ κυρίῳ ἡμῶν.
Syntax: ἐν Χριστῷ Ἰησοῦ may serve (1) as an adjective modifying ζωή 'life', supplying οὖσα 'being', or (2) as an adverb modifying αἰώνιος 'eternal', or (3) as an adverb modifying the verbal idea in χάρισμα 'gift'.
Suggested translations:
For (1) "... but the free gift of God is eternal life (which has been provided) by Christ Jesus our Lord."
"... but the free gift of God is eternal life (which is available through faith) in Christ Jesus our Lord."
For (2) "... but the free gift of God is life lasting forever because of (what) Christ Jesus our Lord (has done)."
For (3) "... but what God has freely and graciously given (through faith) in Christ Jesus our Lord is eternal live."

Romans 8:1
Οὐδὲν ἄρα νῦν κατάκριμα τοῖς ἐν Χριστῷ Ἰησοῦ ...
Syntax: τοῖς ἐν Χριστῷ Ἰησοῦ 'the (ones) in Christ Jesus' is used as a substantive (noun). We may supply οὖσι 'being'.
Suggested translations:
"There is therefore now no condemnation for those who are in (the body of) Christ Jesus ..."
"There is therefore now no condemnation for those (who believe) in Christ Jesus ..."
"Now therefore Christians have no condemnation ..."

Romans 8:2
ὁ γὰρ νόμος τοῦ πνεύματος τῆς ζωῆς ἐν Χριστῷ Ἰησοῦ ἠλευθέρωσέν με ἀπὸ τοῦ νόμου τῆς ἁμαρτίας καὶ τοῦ θανάτου.
Syntax: As an adverb, ἐν Χριστῷ Ἰησοῦ may modify (1) ἠλευθέρωσέν 'set free'. Since ἐν Χριστῷ Ἰησοῦ is not preceded by an article, we cannot be sure that Paul intended this prepositional phrase to modify (2) ζωῆς 'life' as an adjective. This seems to me less likely than (1). To construe

ἐν Χριστῷ Ἰησοῦ adjectivally with (3) πνεύματος 'spirit' or (4) νόμος 'law' seems still less probable.

Suggested translations:

For (1) "For the law of the Spirit of life has set me free by (the power of) Christ Jesus . . ." (or) ". . . has freed me (by faith) in Christ Jesus . . ."

For (2) ". . . the life (which exists) because of (what) Christ Jesus (has done) . . ." (or) ". . . the life (which is a part of the privilege of one) belonging to (the body of) Christ Jesus . . ." (or) ". . . the life (which has its source) in Christ Jesus . . ."

For (3) ". . . the living Spirit (since he was) in Christ Jesus . . ."

For (4) "For (operating) with (the power) of Christ Jesus the law of the Spirit of life has set me free . . ."

Romans 8:39

. . . οὔτε ὕψωμα οὔτε βάθος οὔτε τις κτίσις ἑτέρα δυνήσεται ἡμᾶς χωρίσαι **ἀπὸ τῆς ἀγάπης τοῦ θεοῦ τῆς ἐν Χριστῷ Ἰησοῦ τῷ κυρίῳ ἡμῶν.**

Syntax: ἐν Χριστῷ Ἰησοῦ τῷ κυρίῳ ἡμῶν serves as an adjective in restrictive attributive position modifying ἀγάπης 'love'. We may supply οὔσης 'being'.

Suggested translations:

". . . from the love that God has (for us as it was demonstrated) in (what) Christ Jesus our Lord (did for us)."

". . . from the love that God has for us which (operates) through Christ Jesus our Lord."

Romans 9:1

Ἀλήθειαν λέγω ἐν Χριστῷ, οὐ ψεύδομαι, συμμαρτυρούσης μοι τῆς συνειδήσεώς μου ἐν πνεύματι ἁγίῳ . . .

Syntax: ἐν Χριστῷ can be taken (1) as an adverbial modifier of λέγω 'I speak', or (2) as a substantive in apposition with the subject of λέγω.

Suggested translations:

For (1) "Christ (is my witness), as well as my conscience directed by the Holy Spirit, that I am speaking the truth; I am not lying . . ."

"With Christ (as my witness) . . . I am speaking the truth . . ."

For (2) "(As a man) in (the body of) Christ, I am speaking the truth . . ."

"As a Christian I am speaking the truth . . ."

Remarks: After comparing Matt. 5:34–36 and Rev. 10:6 for the use of ἐν with ὄμνυμι 'I swear', and 2 Cor. 2:17 and 12:19 for ἐν with λαλέω 'I speak', my preference is (1). Furthermore, the context in Rom. 9:3 is harmonious with considering 9:1 to be a strong affirmation.

Romans 12:5
... οὕτως οἱ πολλοὶ ἓν σῶμά ἐσμεν ἐν Χριστῷ, τὸ δὲ καθ' εἷς ἀλλήλων μέλη.
Syntax: ἐν Χριστῷ serves as an adverb modifying ἐσμεν 'we are'.
Suggested translations:
"... so we the many (members) make up one body (because we are united) with Christ ..."
"... so we the many (members) make up one body (because of the work done) by Christ ..."
(CBW) "... so we, (though) many, are (united in) one body (through union) with Christ ..."

Romans 14:14
οἶδα καὶ πέπεισμαι ἐν κυρίῳ Ἰησοῦ ὅτι οὐδὲν κοινὸν δι' ἑαυτοῦ ...
Syntax: ἐν Χριστῷ Ἰησοῦ may be considered (1) as an adverb modifying πέπεισμαι 'I am convinced', or (2) as a substantive meaning '(a person) in Christ' in apposition with the subject of πέπεισμαι.
Suggested translations:
For (1) "... I am convinced by the Lord Jesus ..."
For (2) (NIV) "(As one who is) in the Lord Jesus, I am fully convinced ..."
"... as a Christian I am convinced ..."

Romans 15:17
ἔχω οὖν τὴν καύχησιν ἐν Χριστῷ Ἰησοῦ τὰ πρὸς τὸν θεόν ...
Syntax: ἐν Χριστῷ Ἰησοῦ may be considered (1) an adverbial modifier of ἔχω 'have', (2) an adverbial modifier of the verbal idea in καύχησιν 'boasting', or (3) a substantive in apposition with the subject of ἔχω.
Suggested translations:
For (1) "So Christ Jesus is the source of my boasting about the (work which I have done) for God ..."
For (2) "So in what pertains to God I may boast in (the work done by) Christ Jesus ..."
(BGD) "[So] I may boast in Christ of my relation to God."
For (3) (CBW) "So, as a Christian, I am proud of the things that I have done for God ..."

Romans 16:2
... ἵνα αὐτὴν προσδέξησθε ἐν κυρίῳ ἀξίως τῶν ἁγίων ...
Syntax: ἐν κυρίῳ may be considered (1) a substantive meaning '(people) in Christ' in apposition with the subject of προσδέξησθε 'you welcome', or (2) a substantive in apposition with αὐτήν 'her'.
Suggested translations:
For (1) "... that you (as believers) in the Lord welcomed her as saints should be welcomed ..."
For (2) "... that you welcome her as a (sister) believing in the Lord as saints should be welcomed ..."

Romans 16:3
Ἀσπάσασθε Πρίσκαν καὶ Ἀκύλαν τοὺς συνεργούς μου ἐν Χριστῷ Ἰησοῦ ...
Syntax: ἐν Χριστῷ Ἰησοῦ may be considered (1) an adjectival phrase modifying συνεργούς 'fellow workers' and we may supply τοὺς ὄντας '(those who) are', (2) an adverbial phrase modifying ἀσπάσασθε 'greet', or (3) a substantival expression meaning 'people in Christ Jesus' in apposition with the subject of ἀσπάσασθε 'greet'. Compare Rom. 16:9.
Suggested translations:
For (1) "Greet Prisca and Aquila my fellow workers in (the cause of) Christ Jesus."
(CBW) "Greet Pricsa and Aquila my fellow workers in (the work of) Christ Jesus ..."
"... my Christian fellow workers ..."
For (2) "Greet in a Christian manner Prisca and Aquila my fellow workers ..."
For (3) "As Christians you should greet Prisca and Aquila my fellow workers."
Remark: Because of the position of ἐν Χριστῷ Ἰησοῦ after συνεργούς μου 'my fellow workers', I prefer (1).

Romans 16:7
ἀσπάσασθε Ἀνδρόνικον καὶ Ἰουνιᾶν τοὺς συγγενεῖς μου καὶ συναιχμαλώτους μου, οἵτινές εἰσιν ἐπίσημοι ἐν τοῖς ἀποστόλοις, οἳ καὶ πρὸ ἐμοῦ γέγοναν ἐν Χριστῷ.
Syntax: ἐν Χριστῷ is an adverbial modifier of γέγοναν meaning 'were in Christ', 'have been in Christ', or 'came to be in Christ'.
Suggested translations:
"... who also were Christians before I was."

(LB) "... (who also) became Christians before I did."
"... who became (members of the body) of Christ before me."

Romans 16:8
ἀσπάσασθε Ἀμπλιᾶτον τὸν ἀγαπητόν μου ἐν κυρίῳ.
Syntax: ἐν κυρίῳ may be considered (1) an adverb modifying ἀσπάσασθε 'greet', or (2) a substantive, meaning '(a person) in Christ' in apposition with the subject of ἀσπάσασθε 'greet', supplying οἱ ὄντες '(who) are' or (3) an adverb modifying the verbal idea in ἀγαπητόν 'loved'.
Suggested translations:
For (1) "Greet Ampliatus ... in a Christian way."
For (2) "(As people belonging) to the Lord greet Ampliatus my dear friend."
For (3) "Greet Ampliatus (whom) I love (because he is) a believer."

Romans 16:9
ἀσπάσασθε Οὐρβανὸν τὸν συνεργὸν ἡμῶν ἐν Χριστῷ ...
Syntax: ἐν Χριστῷ may be (1) an adjectival modifier of συνεργόν 'fellow worker', supplying τὸν ὄντα '(who) is', (2) an adverbial modifier of ἀσπάσασθε 'greet', or (3) a substantival expression in apposition with the subject of ἀσπάσασθε 'greet'. Compare Rom 16:3.
Suggested translations:
For (1) "Remember me to Urbanus, my fellow worker in (the cause of) Christ."
(CBW) "... my fellow worker in (the work of) Christ"
"... my Christian fellow worker."
For (2) "In a Christian manner greet Urbanus my fellow worker."
"Greet Urbanus my fellow worker, as Christians (should greet one another)."
For (3) "As Christians, greet Urbanus my fellow worker."
Remark: Because of the position of ἐν Χριστῷ after συνεργὸν ἡμῶν 'our fellow worker', I prefer (1).

Romans 16:10
ἀσπάσασθε Ἀπελλῆν τὸν δόκιμον ἐν Χριστῷ.
Syntax: ἐν Χριστῷ may be (1) a substantival expression which with τὸν δόκιμον 'the esteemed' is an appositive to Ἀπελλῆν 'Apelles', or (2) an adverbial expression modifying δόκιμον 'esteemed' to limit the extent of the approval expressed (so Kittel). We may supply ὄντα '(who) is'.

Suggested translations:
For (1) "Remember me to Apelles, that most venerated Christian."
For (2) "Greet Apelles, who is esteemed (respected) in (his) Christ(ian life)."

Romans 16:11
ἀσπάσασθε τοὺς ἐκ τῶν Ναρκίσσου τοὺς ὄντας ἐν κυρίῳ.
Syntax: ἐν κυρίῳ serves as an adverb modifying τοὺς ὄντας '(who) are'.
Suggested translations:
"Greet those of Narcissus' household who are believers." or
"... who are Christians."

Romans 16:12a
ἀσπάσασθε Τρύφαιναν καὶ Τρυφῶσαν τὰς κοπιώσας ἐν κυρίῳ.
Syntax: ἐν κυρίῳ serves as an adverb modifying κοπιώσας '(who) have worked.'
Suggested translations:
"... who have worked hard with (the strength of) the Lord."
"... who have worked hard in (the service of) the Lord."

Romans 16:12b
ἀσπάσασθε Περσίδα τὴν ἀγαπητήν, ἥτις πολλὰ ἐκοπίασεν ἐν κυρίῳ.
Syntax: ἐν κυρίῳ serves as an adverb modifying ἐκοπίασεν 'she worked'.
Suggested translations:
"Greet Persis the dear sister, who has worked very hard with (the strength of) the Lord."
"... in (the service of) the Lord."

Romans 16:22
ἀσπάζομαι ὑμᾶς ἐγὼ Τέρτιος ὁ γράψας τὴν ἐπιστολὴν ἐν κυρίῳ.
Syntax: ἐν κυρίῳ may be considered (1) an adverb modifying ἀσπάζομαι 'I greet', or (2) a substantive, meaning '(a person) in Christ' in apposition with ἐγὼ Τέρτιος 'I Tertius', or (3) an adverb modifying γράψας 'having written'.
Suggested translations:
For (1) "I Tertius greet you as a believer should, I who wrote down this epistle."
For (2) "I Tertius, a believer, who wrote down this epistle, greet you."
For (3) "I Tertius who wrote down this epistle, in (service to) the Lord, send you my greetings."

1 Corinthians 1:2
... τῇ ἐκκλησίᾳ τοῦ θεοῦ τῇ οὔσῃ ἐν Κορίνθῳ, ἡγιασμένοις ἐν Χριστῷ Ἰησοῦ ...
Syntax: ἐν Χριστῷ Ἰησοῦ may be considered (1) adverbial modifying ἡγιασμένοις 'sanctified', meaning 'sanctified by Christ Jesus', or (2) substantival modified by ἡγιασμένοις 'sanctified', ἐν Χριστῷ Ἰησοῦ meaning '(people) in Christ Jesus.'
Suggested translations:
For (1) "... (people) sanctified by (the power of) Christ Jesus ..."
"... (people) sanctified by (being united with) Christ Jesus ..."
"... (people) sanctified (by faith) in Christ Jesus ..."
For (2) "... sanctified Christians ..."

1 Corinthians 1:4
Εὐχαριστῶ τῷ θεῷ μου πάντοτε περὶ ὑμῶν ἐπὶ τῇ χάριτι τοῦ θεοῦ τῇ δοθείσῃ ὑμῖν ἐν Χριστῷ Ἰησοῦ ...
Syntax: ἐν Χριστῷ Ἰησοῦ may be considered (1) adverbial modifying δοθείσῃ 'given', or (2) substantival in apposition with ὑμῖν 'you', ἐν Χριστῷ Ἰησοῦ meaning '(people) in Christ Jesus'. We may supply οὖσι '(who) are'.
Suggested translations:
For (1) "... for the grace of God given to you (because you) belong to (the body of) Christ Jesus ..."
"... for the grace of God given to you by (the power of) Christ Jesus ..."
"... for the grace of God given to you (because of the work done) by Christ Jesus ..."
"... for the grace of God given to you (when you were made members of the body) of Christ Jesus ..."
For (2) "... for the grace of God given to you (who are members of the body) of Christ Jesus ..."

1 Corinthians 1:5
... ὅτι ἐν παντὶ ἐπλουτίσθητε ἐν αὐτῷ ...
Syntax: ἐν αὐτῷ 'in him' may be considered an adverb modifying ἐπλουτίσθητε 'you have been enriched' or (2) a substantive meaning '(people) in Christ', in apposition with the subject of ἐπλουτίσθητε.
Suggested translations:
For (1) "... because you have been enriched by him ..."
For (2) "... because (as believers) in him you have been enriched."

1 Corinthians 1:30
ἐξ αὐτοῦ δὲ ὑμεῖς ἐστε ἐν Χριστῷ Ἰησοῦ . . .
Syntax: ἐν Χριστῷ Ἰησοῦ may be considered (1) adverbial modifying ἐστε 'you are', or (2) substantival ('people in Christ Jesus') serving as a predicate nominative after ἐστε 'you are'.
Suggested translations:
For (1) "Now because of him you are (united) with Christ Jesus . . ."
"Now because of him you have (true) existence (by faith) in Christ Jesus . . ."
For (2) "Now because of him you are (members of the body) of Christ Jesus . . ."

1 Corinthians 1:31
ἵνα καθὼς γέγραπται, Ὁ καυχώμενος ἐν κυρίῳ καυχάσθω.
Syntax: ἐν κυρίῳ may be considered (1) an adverb modifying καυχάσθω, 'let him boast', or (2) a substantive meaning '(a person) in the Lord' in apposition with the subject of καυχάσθω.
Suggested translations:
For (1) ". . . Let the one who boasts boast (because of what the) Lord (has done)."
For (2) ". . . Let the one who boasts boast (as one who belongs to the) Lord."

1 Corinthians 3:1
Κἀγώ, ἀδελφοί, οὐκ ἠδυνήθην λαλῆσαι ὑμῖν ὡς πνευματικοῖς ἀλλ' ὡς σαρκίνοις, ὡς νηπίοις ἐν Χριστῷ.
Syntax: ἐν Χριστῷ may be (1) substantival, meaning '(people) in Christ', or (2) adverbial modifying νηπίοις 'babes' (so Kittel).
Suggested translations:
For (1) ". . . as to immature Christians."
(CBW) ". . . as to mere baby Christians."
For (2) ". . . as to (those who are) immature in (their) Christ(ian lives)."

1 Corinthians 4:10
ἡμεῖς μωροὶ διὰ Χριστόν, ὑμεῖς δὲ φρόνιμοι ἐν Χριστῷ . . .
Syntax: ἐν Χριστῷ may be (1) substantival, meaning '(people) in Christ', or (2) adverbial, modifying φρόνιμοι 'sensible' (so Kittel). We may supply ἐστε 'you are'.
Suggested translations:
For (1) ". . . but you (are) sensible (prudent, wise) Christians . . ."
For (2) ". . . but you (are) sensible (prudent, wise) in (your) Christ(ian lives) . . ."

1 Corinthians 4:15a
ἐὰν γὰρ μυρίους παιδαγωγοὺς ἔχητε ἐν Χριστῷ, ἀλλ' οὐ πολλοὺς πατέρας . . .
Syntax: ἐν Χριστῷ may be (1) adverbial modifying ἔχητε 'you have', or (2) adjectival modifying παιδαγωγούς 'tutors'.
Suggested translations:
For (1) ". . . for if you have countless tutors among Christ(ians) (or) in (the) Christ(ian church), yet you do not have many fathers . . ."
For (2) "for if you have countless Christian tutors . . ."
"for if you have countless tutors (to lead you on) in (the) Christ(ian life) . . ."

1 Corinthians 4:15b
. . . ἐν γὰρ Χριστῷ Ἰησοῦ διὰ τοῦ εὐαγγελίου ἐγὼ ὑμᾶς ἐγέννησα.
Syntax: ἐν Χριστῷ Ἰησοῦ is an adverbial expression modifying ἐγέννησα 'became a father'.
Suggested translations:
". . . for by (the power) of Christ Jesus through the Gospel I became your father."
". . . for (because of the work done) by Christ I became your father through the Gospel."

1 Corinthians 4:17a
. . . Τιμόθεον, ὅς ἐστίν μου τέκνον ἀγαπητὸν καὶ πιστὸν ἐν κυρίῳ . . .
Syntax: ἐν κυρίῳ may be considered (1) an adverb modifying ἀγαπητόν 'loved', and πιστόν 'reliable', or (2) a substantive, meaning '(a person) in the Lord' modified by ἀγαπητόν and πιστόν.
Suggested translations:
For (1) ". . . Timothy, who is my child, loved and reliable (because of what the) Lord (has done for him) . . ."
For (2) ". . . Timothy, who is my child, a loved and trustworthy (believer) in the Lord . . ."

1 Corinthians 4:17b
. . . ὃς ὑμᾶς ἀναμνήσει τὰς ὁδούς μου τὰς ἐν Χριστῷ Ἰησοῦ, καθὼς πανταχοῦ ἐν πάσῃ ἐκκλησίᾳ διδάσκω.
Syntax: ἐν Χριστῷ Ἰησοῦ is an adjectival expression in restrictive attributive position modifying ὁδούς 'ways'. We may supply οὔσας '(which) are'. The idea of διδάσκω 'I teach' may color ὁδούς 'ways' to the point of making it mean 'teachings', or 'methods'.

Suggested translations
>(BAGD) ". . . my Christian teachings . . ."
>(CBW) ". . . my methods in (the work of) Christ Jesus . . ."
>(NEB) ". . . the way of life in Christ which I follow . . ."
>". . . the way I live the Christian life . . ."

1 Corinthians 7:22
ὁ γὰρ ἐν κυρίῳ κληθεὶς δοῦλος ἀπελεύθερος κυρίου ἐστίν . . .
Syntax: ἐν κυρίῳ modifies κληθείς 'called' as an adverb.
Suggested translation:
>"For the slave who has been called by the Lord is the Lord's freedman. . ."

1 Corinthians 7:39
. . . ἐὰν δὲ κοιμηθῇ ὁ ἀνήρ, ἐλευθέρα ἐστὶν ᾧ θέλει γαμηθῆναι, μόνον ἐν κυρίῳ.
Syntax: ἐν κυρίῳ serves as a substantive meaning '(a person) in the Lord'. We may supply τῷ ὄντι '(one who) is' to parallel the structure of ᾧ 'to whom' before θέλει 'she wishes'.
Suggested translation:
>". . . but if her husband dies, she is free to be married to the one she wishes, (but) only (to the one who is a believer) in the Lord."

1 Corinthians 9:1
οὐ τὸ ἔργον μου ὑμεῖς ἐστε ἐν κυρίῳ;
Syntax: ἐν κυρίῳ may be considered (1) an adverb modifying the verbal idea in ἔργον 'work' or (2) a substantive meaning '(people) in the Lord', in apposition with τὸ ἔργον 'the work'.
Suggested translations:
For (1) "Are you not the work I (have done by the strength of the) Lord?"
For (2) "(As people who believe) in the Lord, are you not my work?"

1 Corinthians 9:2
. . . ἡ γὰρ σφραγίς μου τῆς ἀποστολῆς ὑμεῖς ἐστε ἐν κυρίῳ.
Syntax: ἐν κυρίῳ may be considered (1) an adverb modifying ἐστε 'you are', or (2) an adverb modifying the verbal idea in ἀποστολῆς 'apostleship', or (3) a substantive, meaning '(people) in the Lord', in apposition with ὑμεῖς 'you'.

Suggested translations:
For (1) "For you are the seal (i.e. the proof) of my apostleship (i.e. of my being sent to preach the gospel) (because you are) Christians.
For (2) "For you are the evidence that I have been sent by the Lord."
For (3) "For you as people united with the Lord are the evidence that I have been sent."

1 Corinthians 11:11
πλὴν οὔτε γυνὴ χωρὶς ἀνδρὸς οὔτε ἀνὴρ χωρὶς γυναικὸς ἐν κυρίῳ . . .
Syntax: ἐν κυρίῳ is an adverb modifying ἐστι 'is', supplied twice.
Suggested translation:
"At any rate, in the Lord's (sight) woman (is) not independent of man, nor (is) man independent of woman."

1 Corinthians 15:18
ἄρα καὶ οἱ κοιμηθέντες ἐν Χριστῷ ἀπώλοντο.
Syntax: ἐν Χριστῷ may be considered (1) substantival, meaning '(people) in Christ' or (2) adverbial modifying κοιμηθέντες 'have fallen asleep'.
Suggested translations:
For (1) "Then also the Christians who have died have perished."
For (2) (CBW) "Yes, even those who have fallen asleep, though in (union with) Christ, have perished."

1 Corinthians 15:19
εἰ ἐν τῇ ζωῇ ταύτῃ ἐν Χριστῷ ἠλπικότες ἐσμὲν μόνον, ἐλεεινότεροι πάντων ἀνθρώπων ἐσμέν.
Syntax: ἐν Χριστῷ may be considered (1) adverbial modifying ἠλπικότες ἐσμέν 'having hoped' or (2) substantival meaning '(people) in Christ' in apposition with the subject of ἠλπικότες ἐσμέν 'having hoped'.
Suggested translations:
For (1) "If in this life only we have placed our hope in Christ, we are more to be pitied than all (other) people."
For (2) "If we Christians have entertained hope only during this life..."

1 Corinthians 15:22
ὥσπερ γὰρ ἐν τῷ Ἀδὰμ πάντες ἀποθνῄσκουσιν, οὕτως καὶ ἐν τῷ Χριστῷ πάντες ζῳοποιηθήσονται.

Syntax: ἐν Χριστῷ may be (1) adverbial modifying ζῳοποιηθήσονται 'will be made alive', or (2) substantival meaning '(people) in Christ' serving as subject of ζῳοποιηθήσονται 'will be made alive'.
Suggested translations:
For (1) "for just as all die because of Adam, so all will be made alive because of the Messiah."
For (2) "for just as all who are related to Adam die, so also all who are united with Christ will be made alive."

1 Corinthians 15:31
καθ' ἡμέραν ἀποθνῄσκω, νὴ τὴν ὑμετέραν καύχησιν, ἀδελφοί, ἣν ἔχω ἐν Χριστῷ Ἰησοῦ τῷ κυρίῳ ἡμῶν.
Syntax: ἐν Χριστῷ Ἰησοῦ τῷ κυρίῳ ἡμῶν may be (1) adverbial modifying ἔχω 'have', or (2) substantival, meaning '(a man) in Christ Jesus our Lord', in apposition with the subject of ἔχω 'have'.
Suggested translations:
For (1) "... by the boasting about you, brothers, which I have in (the work accomplished among you by) Christ Jesus our Lord."
For (2) "... by the boasting about you, brothers, which I as a Christian have."
Remarks: Note that ὑμετέραν 'your', stands in place of ὑμῶν 'of you' either (1) as an objective genitive, or (2) as a subjective genitive. The two following translations result: (1) "I rejoice over you." (2) "You rejoice over me." (1) fits the present context.
A great deal is packed into this verse: (1) Paul affirms that he is facing death every day. (2) He wishes to make this affirmation very emphatic. (3) He is proud of the Corinthian believers. (4) His pride, however, is tempered by his relation to Christ Jesus. (5) Assuming his pride or rejoicing in the Corinthian believers to be well-known, Paul makes this fact the basis of his solemn protestation. The whole thought may be paraphrased thus:
"Every day I face death. I boast about you Corinthians. Christ Jesus our Lord has done and is doing a work of grace in you. Let the fact of my boasting about the Lord's work in you stand as a witness to the truth of my declaration that I face the danger of death every day." The same idea may be put more succinctly: "As surely as I boast about the Lord's work in you, brothers, I face death daily."

1 Corinthians 15:58
... ὁ κόπος ὑμῶν οὐκ ἔστιν κενὸς ἐν κυρίῳ.
Syntax: ἐν κυρίῳ serves as an adverb modifying ἔστιν 'is'.
Suggested translation:
"... your labor is not without result (because it is done) in the Lord's (strength)" or "... with the Lord's (blessing)."

1 Corinthians 16:19
ἀσπάζεται ὑμᾶς ἐν κυρίῳ πολλὰ Ἀκύλας καὶ Πρίσκα σὺν τῇ κατ' οἶκον αὐτῶν ἐκκλησίᾳ.
Syntax: ἐν κυρίῳ may be considered (1) an adverb modifying ἀσπάζεται or (2) a substantive, meaning '(people) in the Lord', in apposition with ὑμᾶς 'you'.
Suggested translations:
For (1) "Aquila and Priscilla greet you warmly (as the people) of the Lord (should be greeted) ..."
For (2) "Aquila and Priscilla greet you warmly (as people who belong) to the Lord ..."

1 Corinthians 16:24
ἡ ἀγάπη μου μετὰ πάντων ὑμῶν ἐν Χριστῷ Ἰησοῦ.
Syntax: ἐν Χριστῷ Ἰησοῦ seems to be used as a substantival expression in apposition with ὑμῶν 'you'. We may supply τῶν ὄντων '(those who) are'.
Suggested translation:
"My love (will be) with all of you Christians."

2 Corinthians 1:19
ὁ τοῦ θεοῦ γὰρ υἱὸς Ἰησοῦς Χριστὸς ὁ ἐν ὑμῖν δι' ἡμῶν κηρυχθείς ... οὐκ ἐγένετο Ναὶ καὶ Οὔ, ἀλλὰ Ναὶ ἐν αὐτῷ γέγονεν.
Syntax: ἐν αὐτῷ 'in him' serves as an adverb modifying γέγονεν 'proved to be'.
Suggested translations:
"For the gospel of the Son of God Jesus Christ who was preached among you by us ... did not prove to be (an uncertain statement in which we said) "Yes" and (meant) "No", but it is (a statement) by him (meaning) "Yes"."
"... it is (a statement made) in his (integrity) ..."
"... it is (a message delivered) with his (authority) ..."

2 Corinthians 1:20
ὅσαι γὰρ ἐπαγγελίαι θεοῦ, ἐν αὐτῷ τὸ Ναί ...
Syntax: ἐν αὐτῷ 'in him' serves as an adverb to modify γέγονεν 'is', to be supplied from verse 19.

Suggested translations:
> "For however many God's promises (are), (they are) 'Yes' (as spoken) with his (authority)."
> ". . . with his (integrity)."

2 Corinthians 2:12
. . . καὶ θύρας μοι ἀνεῳγμένης ἐν κυρίῳ . . .
Syntax: ἐν κυρίῳ 'serves as an adverb modifying ἀνεῳγμένης 'opened'.
Suggested translation:
> ". . . and although a door (of opportunity) had been opened by the Lord for me . . ."

2 Corinthians 2:14
Τῷ δὲ θεῷ χάρις τῷ πάντοτε θριαμβεύοντι ἡμᾶς ἐν τῷ Χριστῷ . . .
Syntax: ἐν τῷ Χριστῷ is adverbial modifying θριαμβεύοντι 'leads in triumph'.
Suggested translations:
> "Thanks be to God who always leads us in a triumphal procession (as captives) of Christ . . ."
> "Thanks be to God who always gives us a triumphal procession because of the victory which Christ has won . . ."
> "Thanks be to God who always exhibits us in a public procession as trophies belonging to Christ . . ."

2 Corinthians 2:17
οὐ γάρ ἐσμεν ὡς οἱ πολλοὶ καπηλεύοντες τὸν λόγον τοῦ θεοῦ, ἀλλ' ὡς ἐξ εἰλικρινείας, ἀλλ' ὡς ἐκ θεοῦ κατέναντι θεοῦ ἐν Χριστῷ λαλοῦμεν.
Syntax: ἐν Χριστῷ may be considered (1) adverbial modifying λαλοῦμεν 'speak', or (2) substantival in apposition with the subject of λαλοῦμεν 'speak'.
Suggested translations:
For (1) ". . . indeed, as (sent) from God in the presence of God we speak with Christ (as our witness)."
> ". . . yes, even as (messengers) from God we are speaking in the presence of God with (the power of) Christ."

For (2) ". . . yes, even as (messengers) from God we speak as Christians in the presence of God." See *Remarks* on Rom. 9:1.

2 Corinthians 3:14

ἀλλὰ ἐπωρώθη τὰ νοήματα αὐτῶν. ἄχρι γὰρ τῆς σήμερον ἡμέρας τὸ αὐτὸ κάλυμμα ἐπὶ τῇ ἀναγνώσει τῆς παλαιᾶς διαθήκης μένει μὴ ἀνακαλυπτόμενον, **ὅτι ἐν Χριστῷ καταργεῖται** . . .

Syntax: In 2 Cor. 3:14, the subject of καταργεῖται 'is removed' may be ἡ παλαιὰ διαθήκη 'the old covenant', or, more probably, κάλυμμα 'veil'. In that case, the meaning is 'removed'. So BAGD. In either case, ἐν Χριστῷ serves as an adverb modifying καταργεῖται 'is removed'.

Suggested translations:

". . . because (the veil) is removed (by faith) in Christ . . ."

". . . because (the veil) is removed (by believing) in Christ."

2 Corinthians 5:17

ὥστε **εἴ τις ἐν Χριστῷ**, καινὴ κτίσις· τὰ ἀρχαῖα παρῆλθεν, ἰδοὺ γέγονεν καινά . . .

Syntax: ἐν Χριστῷ may be considered (1) adverbial modifying ἐστί 'is', or ἐγένετο 'has become' to be supplied, or (2) substantival, meaning '(a person) in Christ' serving as the predicate of ἐστί 'is' understood.

Suggested translations:

For (1) ". . . if anyone (has been made a member of the body) of Christ . . ."

". . . if anyone (has become) a Christian . . ."

For (2) ". . . if anyone (is) a Christian . . ."

". . . if anyone (is) (a member of the body) of Christ . . ."

". . . if anyone (is united with) Christ . . ."

2 Corinthians 5:19

. . . ὡς ὅτι θεὸς ἦν ἐν Χριστῷ κόσμον καταλλάσσων ἑαυτῷ . . .

Syntax: ἐν Χριστῷ is adverbial modifying (1) ἦν 'was' alone, or (2) ἦν . . . καταλλάσσων 'was reconciling' taken as a periphrastic imperfect indicative.

Suggested translations:

For (1) ". . . that God was (working) through Christ when He was reconciling the world to himself . . ."

For (2) ". . . that God was reconciling the world to himself (by working) through Christ . . ."

". . . that God in (the person of) Christ was reconciling the world to himself . . ."

2 Corinthians 5:21
... ἵνα ἡμεῖς γενώμεθα δικαιοσύνη θεοῦ ἐν αὐτῷ.
Syntax: ἐν αὐτῷ 'in him' serves as an adverb modifying γενώμεθα 'we might become'.
Suggested translations:
"... that we might become God's righteousness (because of what Christ has done)."
"... righteousness (by becoming a part of his body)."

2 Corinthians 10:17
Ὁ δὲ καυχώμενος ἐν κυρίῳ καυχάσθω ...
Syntax and suggested translations are the same as for 1 Cor. 1:31.

2 Corinthians 12:2
οἶδα ἄνθρωπον ἐν Χριστῷ πρὸ ἐτῶν δεκατεσσάρων ... ἁρπαγέντα τὸν τοιοῦτον ἕως τρίτου οὐρανοῦ.
Syntax: ἐν Χριστῷ seems to be adjectival modifying ἄνθρωπον 'man'. We may supply ὄντα 'being'.
Suggested translations:
"I know that a Christian fourteen years ago ... that such a man was caught up to the third heaven."
"I know that a man (who was a member of the body) of Christ fourteen years ago ..."

2 Corinthians 12:19
Πάλαι δοκεῖτε ὅτι ὑμῖν ἀπολογούμεθα. κατέναντι θεοῦ ἐν Χριστῷ λαλοῦμεν· τὰ δὲ πάντα, ἀγαπητοί, ὑπὲρ τῆς ὑμῶν οἰκοδομῆς.
Syntax: (1) We may consider that λαλοῦμεν 'we speak' has two adverbial modifiers, κατέναντι θεοῦ 'in the sight of God' and ἐν Χριστῷ, or (2) that οἱ ὄντες '(those who) are' may be supplied, modifying the subject of λαλοῦμεν, or (3) that τοῦ ὄντος '(who) is' may be supplied modifying θεοῦ 'God'. I prefer (1). See *Remarks* on Rom. 9:1.
Suggested translations:
For (1) "In the presence of God we speak with Christ (as our witness)."
"In the presence of God we speak with (the power of) Christ ..."
For (2) "In the presence of God we speak as Christians ..." (or if the first person plural is taken as an editorial 'we' or as a reference to himself by Paul with a polite inclusion of Titus), "In the presence of God I speak as a Christian ..."
For (3) "In the presence of God who is in Christ we speak ..."

2 Corinthians 13:4
καὶ γὰρ ἡμεῖς ἀσθενοῦμεν ἐν αὐτῷ . . .

Syntax: ἐν αὐτῷ 'in him' may be considered (1) an adverb modifying ἀσθενοῦμεν 'we are weak' or (2) a substantive meaning '(people) in him', in apposition with the subject of ἀσθενοῦμεν.

Suggested translations:

For (1) "(In our identification) with him we are weak . . ."

For (2) "(As people who are) in his (body) we are weak . . ."

Galatians 1:22
ἤμην δὲ ἀγνοούμενος τῷ προσώπῳ ταῖς ἐκκλησίαις τῆς Ἰουδαίας ταῖς ἐν Χριστῷ . . .

Syntax: ἐν Χριστῷ is adjectival modifying ἐκκλησίαις 'churches' in restrictive attributive position.

Suggested translation:

"But I was not know personally to the Christian assemblies in Judea . . ."

Galatians 2:4
. . . διὰ δὲ τοὺς παρεισάκτους ψευδαδέλφους, οἵτινες παρεισῆλθον κατασκοπῆσαι τὴν ἐλευθερίαν ἡμῶν ἣν ἔχομεν ἐν Χριστῷ Ἰησοῦ, ἵνα ἡμᾶς καταδουλώσουσιν . . .

Syntax: ἐν Χριστῷ may be considered (1) adverbial modifying ἔχομεν 'have', or (2) substantival meaning '(people) in Christ Jesus' in apposition with the subject of ἔχομεν 'have'.

Suggested translations:

For (1) ". . . our liberty which we enjoy (i.e., have for our use) (because we have placed our faith) in Christ Jesus . . ."

"our liberty which we enjoy because of (what) Christ Jesus (has done) . . ."

". . . our liberty which we enjoy (because we are united) with Christ Jesus . . ."

For (2) ". . . our liberty which we enjoy as Christians . . ."

Galatians 2:17
εἰ δὲ ζητοῦντες δικαιωθῆναι ἐν Χριστῷ εὑρέθημεν καὶ αὐτοὶ ἁμαρτωλοί, ἆρα Χριστὸς ἁμαρτίας διάκονος; μὴ γένοιτο.

Syntax: ἐν Χριστῷ may be considered (1) adverbial modifying δικαιωθῆναι 'to be justified', expressing agency, or (2) substantival meaning '(people) in Christ' in apposition with the subject of εὑρέθημεν 'we have been found'.

Suggested translations:
For (1) "But if we ourselves also have been found to be sinners although we are trying to be justified (by faith) in Christ, is Christ then a servant of sin? Perish the thought!"

"... justified (because of the work done) by Christ ..."

For (2) "But if we ourselves also as Christians have been found to be sinners although we are trying to be justified, is Christ then a servant of sin? Perish the thought!" (This rendering is really not satisfactory.)

Galatians 3:14
... ἵνα εἰς τὰ ἔθνη ἡ εὐλογία τοῦ Ἀβραὰμ γένηται ἐν Χριστῷ Ἰησοῦ, ἵνα τὴν ἐπαγγελίαν τοῦ πνεύματος λάβωμεν διὰ τῆς πίστεως.
Syntax: ἐν Χριστῷ Ἰησοῦ is adverbial, modifying γένηται 'might come'.
Suggested translations:
"... that the blessing (pronounced upon) Abraham might come to the Gentiles (by faith) in Christ Jesus."
"... might come to the Gentiles (because of the work done) by Christ Jesus."

Galatians 3:26
Πάντες γὰρ υἱοὶ θεοῦ ἐστε διὰ τῆς πίστεως ἐν Χριστῷ Ἰησοῦ.
Syntax: ἐν Χριστῷ Ἰησοῦ is adverbial modifying the idea of believing in πίστεως 'faith.'
Suggested translations:
(WFB) "You are all God's children by believing in Christ Jesus."
(NASB) "For you are all sons of God through faith in Christ Jesus."

Galatians 3:28
... πάντες γὰρ ὑμεῖς εἷς ἐστε ἐν Χριστῷ Ἰησοῦ.
Syntax: ἐν Χριστῷ Ἰησοῦ is adverbial modifying ἐστε 'are'.
Suggested translation:
"... for you are all one (because you have been united) in Christ Jesus."

Galatians 5:6
ἐν γὰρ Χριστῷ Ἰησοῦ οὔτε περιτομή τι ἰσχύει οὔτε ἀκροβυστία, ἀλλὰ πίστις δι' ἀγάπης ἐνεργουμένη.
Syntax: ἐν Χριστῷ Ἰησοῦ is adverbial modifying ἰσχύει 'avails'.

Suggested translations:
"For in (our relationship to) Christ Jesus neither circumcision nor uncircumcision has any meaning ..."
"For in (the body of) Christ Jesus ..."
"For among Christians ..."

Galatians 5:10
ἐγὼ πέποιθα εἰς ὑμᾶς ἐν κυρίῳ ὅτι οὐδὲν ἄλλο φρονήσετε ...
Syntax: ἐν κυρίῳ serves as an adverb modifying πέποιθα 'I trust'.
Suggested translation:
"I am putting my confidence in the Lord for you that you will have no other view ..."

Ephesians 1:1
Παῦλος ἀπόστολος Χριστοῦ Ἰησοῦ διὰ θελήματος θεοῦ τοῖς ἁγίοις τοῖς οὖσιν ἐν Ἐφέσῳ καὶ πιστοῖς ἐν Χριστῷ Ἰησοῦ ...
Syntax: ἐν Χριστῷ Ἰησοῦ may be considered (1) adverbial modifying πιστοῖς 'faithful', or (2) substantival, meaning '(people) in Christ Jesus', modified by πιστοῖς 'faithful'.
Suggested translations:
For (1) "Paul an apostle of Christ Jesus through the will of God to God's people who are in Ephesus and (who are) trusting in Christ Jesus ..."
For (2) "... and (who are) faithful Christians ..."
"To those in Ephesus who are holy and trustworthy (and who belong) to (the body of) Christ Jesus ..."

Ephesians 1:3
Εὐλογητὸς ὁ θεὸς καὶ πατὴρ τοῦ κυρίου ἡμῶν Ἰησοῦ Χριστοῦ, ὁ εὐλογήσας ἡμᾶς ἐν πάσῃ εὐλογίᾳ πνευματικῇ ἐν τοῖς ἐπουρανίοις ἐν Χριστῷ ...
Syntax: (1) ἐν Χριστῷ may be considered adverbial modifying εὐλογήσας 'has blessed', or (2) adjectival modifying εὐλογίᾳ 'blessing' with τῇ οὔσῃ '(which) is' supplied.
Suggested translations:
For (1) "... who has blessed us with every spiritual blessing in the heavenlies by (making us members of the body of) Christ."
"... who has blessed us with every spiritual blessing in the heavenlies (because of our faith) in Christ ..."
For (2) "... who has blessed us in the heavenlies with every spiritual blessing which is in Christ ..."

Ephesians 1:4
... καθὼς ἐξελέξατο ἡμᾶς ἐν αὐτῷ πρὸ καταβολῆς κόσμου ...
Syntax: ἐν αὐτῷ 'in him' serves as an adverb modifying ἐξελέξατο 'he chose'.
Suggested translations:
"... he chose us (as part of the body of Christ) ..."
"... because of him he chose us ..."

Ephesians 1:6
... εἰς ἔπαινον δόξης τῆς χάριτος αὐτοῦ ἧς ἐχαρίτωσεν ἡμᾶς ἐν τῷ ἠγαπημένῳ.
Syntax: ἐν τῷ ἠγαπημένῳ 'in the beloved' may be considered (1) an adverb modifying ἐχαρίτωσεν "he freely gave', or (2) a substantive if τοὺς ὄντας 'the ones being' is supplied, or (3) and adjective if τῆς οὔσης is supplied.
Suggested translations:
For (1) "... for the praise of the glory of his (i.e., God's) favor with which (God) has blessed us through his beloved (Son)."
"... his favor which he freely gave us along with his Beloved."
"... his favor with which God has blessed us (because we are part of the body of) his Beloved."
For (2) "... his favor which (God) has given us (who are members of the body) of the Beloved."
For (3) "... his favor in the Beloved which (God) has given us."

Ephesians 1:7
ἐν ᾧ ἔχομεν τὴν ἀπολύτρωσιν διὰ τοῦ αἵματος αὐτοῦ ...
Syntax: ἐν ᾧ 'in whom' serves as an adverb modifying ἔχομεν 'we have'.
Suggested translation:
"... because of whom we have redemption ..."
Note: The antecedent of ᾧ 'whom' is τῷ ἀγαπημένῳ in vs. 6, that is, Christ.

Ephesians 1:9
... κατὰ τὴν εὐδοκίαν αὐτοῦ ἣν προέθετο ἐν αὐτῷ ...
Syntax: ἐν αὐτῷ 'in him' serves as an adverb modifying προέθετο 'he proposed'.
Suggested translation:
"... according to his (i.e. God's) pleasure which he (i.e. God) proposed (to accomplish) through him (i.e. Christ) ..."

Ephesians 1:10a
. . . ἀνακεφαλαιώσασθαι τὰ πάντα ἐν τῷ Χριστῷ, τὰ ἐπὶ τοῖς οὐρανοῖς καὶ τὰ ἐπὶ τῆς γῆς . . .
Syntax: ἐν τῷ Χριστῷ is adverbial modifying ἀνακεφαλαιώσασθαι 'to unite'.
Suggested translations:
"... to bring the universe together under (the authority of) Christ ..."
"... to make Christ the supreme ruler of the universe ..."

Ephesians 1:10b
. . . ἀνακεφαλαιώσασθαι τὰ πάντα ἐν τῷ Χριστῷ, τὰ ἐπὶ τοῖς οὐρανοῖς καὶ τὰ ἐπὶ τῆς γῆς **ἐν αὐτῷ**.
Syntax: ἐν αὐτῷ 'in him' serves as an adverb modifying ἀνακεφαλαιώσασθαι 'to unite' just as ἐν τῷ Χριστῷ 'in Christ' does earlier in this verse. The repetition of the reference to Christ is emphatic and αὐτῷ 'him' serves as an antecedent for ᾧ 'whom' in the next verse.
Suggested translation:
"... to bring the universe together under (the authority of) Christ, (that is to bring) the things in the heavens and the things on the earth (together under) his (authority)."

Ephesians 1:11
ἐν ᾧ καὶ ἐκληρώθημεν προορισθέντες κατὰ πρόθεσιν τοῦ τὰ πάντα ἐνεργοῦντος κατὰ τὴν βουλὴν τοῦ θελήματος αὐτοῦ . . .
Syntax: ἐν ᾧ 'in whom' serves as an adverb modifying ἐκληρώθημεν 'we were chosen'.
Suggested translations:
"In whom we also were destined . . ."
"In whom we were also chosen . . ."
(NIV) "In him we were also chosen . . ."
Remark: The third suggestion starts a new sentence at the beginning of vs. 11.

Ephesians 1:12
. . . εἰς τὸ εἶναι **ἡμᾶς** εἰς ἔπαινον δόξης αὐτοῦ **τοὺς προηλπικότας** ἐν **τῷ Χριστῷ** . . .
Syntax: ἐν τῷ Χριστῷ is adverbial modifying προηλπικότας 'hoped before'. Some consider ἡμᾶς 'we' to mean (1) Jewish Christians, or (2) Jews believing in the Messiah; others (3) Christians in general. Suggested translations:
For (1) "... we who have placed our hope in Christ before (the Gentiles did) ..."

For (2) "... we who placed our hope in the Messiah before (he appeared) ..."
For (3) "... we who have placed our hope in Christ before (his full glory is finally revealed) ..."

Ephesians 1:13
ἐν ᾧ καὶ ὑμεῖς ἀκούσαντες τὸν λόγον τῆς ἀληθείας, τὸ εὐαγγέλιον τῆς σωτηρίας ὑμῶν, εν ᾧ καὶ πιστεύσαντες ἐσφραγίσθητε τῷ πνεύματι τῆς ἐπαγγελίας τῷ ἁγίῳ ...

Syntax: (1) The first occurrence of ἐν ᾧ 'in whom' may be an adverbial modifier of a verb to be supplied in this clause, such as ἐγένεσθε 'you came to be', or ἦτε 'you were'. Viewed this way ἀκούσαντες 'having heard' modifies the subject of the supplied verb, and the first ἐν ᾧ 'in whom' in vs. 13 would not be thought of in association with πιστεύσαντες 'having believed' or ἐσφραγίσθητε 'you were sealed'.

(2) The second occurrence of ἐν ᾧ 'in whom' may be a repetition of the first occurrence, to keep the reader's attention on Christ the antecedent of ᾧ. Taken this way the first ἐν ᾧ goes with ἀκούσαντες 'having heard' and the second performs the same function with πιστεύσαντες 'having believed' and ἐσφραγίσθητε 'you were sealed'.

Suggested translations:
For (1) "You also came to be included in Him when you heard the word of truth ..."
"You also were in him because you heard the word of truth ..."
For (2) "... in him (I say) you also believed and were sealed by the promised Holy Spirit ..."

Ephesians 1:15
Διὰ τοῦτο κἀγώ, ἀκούσας τὴν καθ' ὑμᾶς πίστιν ἐν τῷ κυρίῳ Ἰησοῦ καὶ τὴν ἀγάπην τὴν εἰς πάντας τοὺς ἁγίους ...

Syntax: ἐν τῷ κυρίῳ Ἰησοῦ serves as an adverb modifying the verbal idea in πίστιν 'faith'.

Suggested translations:
"... having heard of your faith in the Lord Jesus ..."
"... having heard that you are trusting in the Lord Jesus."

Ephesians 1:20
... ἣν ἐνήργησεν ἐν τῷ Χριστῷ ἐγείρας αὐτὸν ἐκ νεκρῶν καὶ καθίσας ἐν δεξιᾷ αὐτοῦ ἐν τοῖς ἐπουρανίοις ...

Syntax: ἐν τῷ Χριστῷ is adverbial modifying ἐνήργησεν 'brought about'.

Suggested translation:
"... (according to the manifestation of his power) which he brought about in (the physical body of) Christ when he raised him from among the dead ..."

Remark: This is the only instance I have found in this study of a reference to the literal physical body of our Lord.

Ephesians 2:6
... καὶ συνήγειρεν καὶ συνεκάθισεν ἐν τοῖς ἐπουρανίοις ἐν Χριστῷ Ἰησοῦ ...

Syntax: ἐν Χριστῷ Ἰησοῦ is adverbial modifying συνεκάθισεν 'seated with' and probably also συνήγειρεν 'raised up with'.

Suggested translations:
"and he (God) raised (us) with (him) and made (us) to sit with (him) in the heavenlies (since we are members of the body of) Christ Jesus ..."
"... because of (the finished work of) Christ Jesus ..."
"... (by faith) in Christ Jesus ..."

Ephesians 2:7
... ἵνα ἐνδείξηται ἐν τοῖς αἰῶσιν τοῖς ἐπερχομένοις τὸ ὑπερβάλλον πλοῦτος τῆς χάριτος αὐτοῦ ἐν χρηστότητι ἐφ' ἡμᾶς ἐν Χριστῷ Ἰησοῦ.

Syntax: ἐν Χριστῷ Ἰησοῦ may be considered (1) adverbial modifying ἐνδείξηται 'might show', (2) adjectival modifying χρηστότητι 'kindness', or (3) substantival, meaning '(people) in Christ Jesus'.

Suggested translations:
For (1) "... that in the ages to come he (God) might show by (what) Christ Jesus (has done for us) the extraordinary riches of his favor in his kindness to us."
For (2) "... that he (God) might show in the ages to come the extraordinary riches of his favor (manifested) by the kindness of Christ Jesus toward us."
For (3) "... that he (God) might show in the ages to come the extraordinary riches of his favor by his kindness toward us (who are members of the body of) Christ Jesus."

Ephesians 2:10
αὐτοῦ γάρ ἐσμεν ποίημα, κτισθέντες ἐν Χριστῷ Ἰησοῦ ἐπὶ ἔργοις ἀγαθοῖς οἷς προητοίμασεν ὁ θεὸς ἵνα ἐν αὐτοῖς περιπατήσωμεν.
Syntax: ἐν Χριστῷ Ἰησοῦ is adverbial modifying κτισθέντες 'created' to express (1) agency or (2) position.
Suggested translations:
For (1) "For he (God) has made us what we are, because we have been created by Christ Jesus . . ."
"For he (God) has made us what we are, having created us by (the power of) Christ Jesus . . ."
For (2) "For he (God) has made us what we are, having created us (as members of the body of) Christ Jesus . . ."

Ephesians 2:13
νυνὶ δὲ ἐν Χριστῷ Ἰησοῦ ὑμεῖς οἱ ποτε ὄντες μακρὰν ἐγενήθητε ἐγγὺς ἐν τῷ αἵματι τοῦ Χριστοῦ.
Syntax: ἐν Χριστῷ Ἰησοῦ is adverbial modifying ἐγενήθητε 'have come'.
Suggested translations:
"But now (since you have become members of the body of) Christ Jesus, you who were once far off have come to be near because of the blood of Christ."
"But now (by faith) in Christ Jesus . . ."
(CBW) "But now through (your union with) Christ Jesus."

Ephesians 2:15
. . . ἵνα τοὺς δύο κτίσῃ ἐν αὐτῷ εἰς ἕνα καινὸν ἄνθρωπον ποιῶν εἰρήνην . . .
Syntax: ἐν αὐτῷ 'in him' serves as an adverb modifying κτίσῃ 'he might create'.
Suggested translation:
(NIV) "His purpose was to create in himself one new man out of the two, thus making peace . . ."

Ephesians 2:16
. . . ἀποκαταλλάξῃ τοὺς ἀμφοτέρους ἐν ἑνὶ σώματι τῷ θεῷ διὰ τοῦ σταυροῦ, ἀποκτείνας τὴν ἔχθραν ἐν αὐτῷ.
Syntax: ἐν αὐτῷ 'in him' or 'in it' clearly serves as an adverb modifying ἀποκτείνας 'having put to death', but the antecedent of αὐτῷ may be (1) Christ or (2) σταυροῦ 'cross'.
Suggested translations:
For (1) ". . . having put to death their enmity in himself."
For (2) ". . . having put to death their enmity by it (i.e. the cross)."

Ephesians 2:21
... ἐν ᾧ πᾶσα οἰκοδομὴ συναρμολογουμένη αὔξει εἰς ναὸν ἅγιον ἐν κυρίῳ ...
Syntax: (1) ἐν ᾧ 'in whom' serves as an adverb modifying συναρμολογουμένη 'is being joined together'. (2) ἐν κυρίῳ 'in the Lord' serves as an adverb modifying αὔξει 'grows'.
Suggested translation:
"... (1) by whom the whole building is being joined together and (2) by (the work of the) Lord grows into a holy temple."

Ephesians 2:22
... ἐν ᾧ καὶ ὑμεῖς συνοικοδομεῖσθε εἰς κατοικητήριον τοῦ θεοῦ ἐν πνεύματι.
Syntax: ἐν ᾧ 'in whom' serves as an adverb modifying συνοικοδομεῖσθε 'you are being built together'.
Suggested translations:
"... by whom you also are being built together ..."
(NIV) "And in him you too are being built together ..."

Ephesians 3:6
... εἶναι τὰ ἔθνη συγκληρονόμα καὶ σύσσωμα καὶ συμμέτοχα τῆς ἐπαγγελίας ἐν Χριστῷ Ἰησοῦ διὰ τοῦ εὐαγγελίου ...
Syntax: ἐν Χριστῷ Ἰησοῦ is adverbial modifying εἶναι 'to be'.
Suggested translations:
"... that within (the mystical body of) Christ Jesus through the Gospel the Gentiles are fellow heirs and belong to the same body and share the promise (along with Jews who believe) ..."
"... that (by faith) in Christ Jesus ..."
"... that because of (the work of) Christ Jesus ..."

Ephesians 3:11
... κατὰ πρόθεσιν τῶν αἰώνων ἣν ἐποίησεν ἐν τῷ Χριστῷ Ἰησοῦ τῷ κυρίῳ ἡμῶν ...
Syntax: ἐν τῷ Χριστῷ Ἰησοῦ τῷ κυρίῳ ἡμῶν is adverbial modifying ἐποίησεν 'carried out'.
Suggested translations:
"... in accordance with the everlasting plan which he carried out through Christ Jesus our Lord ..."
"... which he carried out (in the work done) by Christ Jesus our Lord ..."

Ephesians 3:12

... ἐν ᾧ ἔχομεν τὴν παρρησίαν καὶ προσαγωγὴν ἐν πεποιθήσει διὰ τῆς πίστεως αὐτοῦ.

Syntax: ἐν ᾧ 'in whom' may be taken (1) as an adverb modifying ἔχομεν 'we have', or (2) as a substantive, meaning '(people) in Christ' in apposition with the subject of ἔχομεν 'we have', or (3) as an adverb modifying the verbal ideas in παρρησίαν 'confidence' and προσαγωγήν 'access'.

Suggested translations:

For (1) "... because of him we have ..."
For (2) "... as members of the body of Christ we have ..."
For (3) "... because of what Christ has done we are joyfully confident as we approach God ..."

Ephesians 3:21

... αὐτῷ ἡ δόξα ἐν τῇ ἐκκλησίᾳ καὶ ἐν Χριστῷ Ἰησοῦ εἰς πάσας τὰς γενεὰς τοῦ αἰῶνος τῶν αἰώνων· ἀμήν.

Syntax: ἐν Χριστῷ Ἰησοῦ is adverbial modifying a verb to be supplied, such as (1) ἔσται 'will be', (2) ἔστω 'be', (3) γένοιτο 'be', or (4) διδόσθω 'be given'.

Suggested translations:

For (1) "... forever and ever the church and Christ Jesus (will be) sources of glory for him (God) ..."
"... he (God) (will have) glory forever and ever because of the church and because of Christ Jesus."
For (2) "... (let) the church and Christ Jesus (be) sources of glory for him (God) forever and ever ..."
For (3) "... (may) the church and Christ Jesus (be) sources of glory for him (God) forever and ever ..."
For (4) "... let glory (be continually given) to him (God) by the church and by Christ Jesus forever and ever ..."

Ephesians 4:1

Παρακαλῶ οὖν ὑμᾶς ἐγὼ ὁ δέσμιος ἐν κυρίῳ ἀξίως περιπατῆσαι τῆς κλήσεως ἧς ἐκλήθητε ...

Syntax: ἐν κυρίῳ may be considered (1) an adverb modifying παρακαλῶ 'I urge', or (2) an adjective modifying δέσμιος 'prisoner', or (3) an adverb modifying the verbal idea in δέσμιος 'prisoner'.

Suggested translations:

For (1) "I a prisoner urge you in (the name of the) Lord ..."
For (2) "I a Christian prisoner urge you ..."
For (3) "I a prisoner bound by the Lord (or) for the Lord ..."

Ephesians 4:17
Τοῦτο οὖν λέγω καὶ μαρτύρομαι ἐν κυρίῳ, μηκέτι ὑμᾶς περιπατεῖν καθὼς καὶ τὰ ἔθνη περιπατεῖ ἐν ματαιότητι τοῦ νοὸς αὐτῶν . . .

Syntax: ἐν κυρίῳ serves (1) as an adverb modifying μαρτύρομαι 'I affirm', and probably λέγω 'I say' also, or (2) as a substantive meaning '(a person) in the Lord' in apposition with the subjects of λέγω 'I say' and μαρτύρομαι 'I affirm'.

Suggested translations:

For (1) "With the Lord as my witness I tell you and implore you not to live any longer as the pagans live in the futility of their thinking . . ."

For (2) "as a believer I tell you . . ."

Ephesians 4:21a
. . . εἴ γε αὐτὸν ἠκούσατε καὶ ἐν αὐτῷ ἐδιδάχθητε . . .

Syntax: ἐν αὐτῷ 'in him' serves (1) as an adverb modifying ἐδιδάχθητε 'you have been taught', or (2) as a substantive meaning '(people) in Christ' in apposition with the subject of ἐδιδάχθητε 'you have been taught'.

Suggested translation:

For (1) ". . . you were taught by him . . ."

". . . you were taught in him (i.e. you received the teaching about him) . . ."

For (2) ". . . as believers you were taught . . ."

Ephesians 4:21b
. . . καθώς ἐστιν ἀλήθεια ἐν τῷ Ἰησοῦ . . .

Syntax: ἐν τῷ Ἰησοῦ serves as an adverb modifying ἐστιν 'is'.

Suggested translations:

(NIV) ". . . in accordance with the truth that is in Jesus."

". . . just as truth exists in Jesus . . ."

Ephesians 4:32
γίνεσθε δὲ εἰς ἀλλήλους χρηστοί, εὔσπλαγχνοι, χαριζόμενοι ἑαυτοῖς καθὼς καὶ ὁ θεὸς ἐν Χριστῷ ἐχαρίσατο ὑμῖν.

Syntax: ἐν Χριστῷ is adverbial modifying ἐχαρίσατο 'has forgiven'.

Suggested translations:

". . . as God also has forgiven you because of Christ."

(LB) ". . . because (you belong to) Christ."

(CBW) ". . . through Christ."

Ephesians 5:8
... ἦτε γάρ ποτε σκότος, νῦν δὲ φῶς ἐν κυρίῳ ...
Syntax: ἐν κυρίῳ may serve (1) as an adverb modifying ἐστε 'you are' to be supplied, or (2) as a substantive meaning '(people) in the Lord' in apposition with the subject of ἐστε 'you are' to be supplied.
Suggested translations:
For (1) "... you are light because you are believers ..."
For (2) "... as believers you are light ..."

Ephesians 6:1
Τὰ τέκνα, ὑπακούετε τοῖς γονεῦσιν ὑμῶν ἐν κυρίῳ ...
Syntax: ἐν κυρίῳ may serve (1) as an adverb modifying ὑπακούετε 'be subject', or (2) as a substantive, meaning '(people) in the Lord' in apposition with the subject of ὑπακούετε 'be subject'.
Suggested translations:
For (1) "... be in submission to your parents because you are believers ..."
For (2) "... as believers in the Lord be subject to your parents ..."

Ephesians 6:10
Τοῦ λοιποῦ, ἐνδυναμοῦσθε ἐν κυρίῳ καὶ ἐν τῷ κράτει τῆς ἰσχύος αὐτοῦ.
Syntax: ἐν κυρίῳ serves as an adverb modifying ἐνδυναμοῦσθε 'be strengthened', which may be either (1) middle or (2) passive.
Suggested translations:
For (1) "... strengthen yourselves continually in (dependence on) the Lord ..."
"... strengthen yourselves continually (with the thought that you are a part of) the Lord's (body) ..."
For (2) "... be continually strengthened by the Lord ..."
"... be continually strengthened by (your union with) the Lord ..."

Ephesians 6:21
Ἵνα δὲ εἰδῆτε καὶ ὑμεῖς τὰ κατ' ἐμέ, τί πράσσω, πάντα γνωρίσει ὑμῖν Τύχικος ὁ ἀγαπητὸς ἀδελφὸς καὶ πιστὸς διάκονος ἐν κυρίῳ ...
Syntax: ἐν κυρίῳ may serve (1) as an adverb modifying πιστός 'trusting', or (2) as an adjective modifying διάκονος 'helper', or (3) as a substantive modifying διάκονος 'helper'.
Suggested translations:
For (1) "... Tychicus ... a helper trusting in the Lord ..."
For (2) "... Tychicus ... a faithful believing helper ..."

For (3) "... Tychicus ... a reliable helper, a believer ..."

Philippians 1:1
Παῦλος καὶ Τιμόθεος δοῦλοι Χριστοῦ Ἰησοῦ πᾶσιν τοῖς ἁγίοις ἐν Χριστῷ Ἰησοῦ τοῖς οὖσιν ἐν Φιλίπποις σὺν ἐπισκόποις καὶ διακόνοις ...

Syntax: ἐν Χριστῷ Ἰησοῦ may be considered (1) adverbial modifying ἁγίοις 'saints', or (2) substantival, meaning '(people) in Christ Jesus' modified by ἁγίοις 'saints'.

Suggested translations:
For (1) "... to all the upright because of Christ Jesus ..."
"... To all God's people (united) in Christ Jesus ..."
For (2) "... to all the upright Christians ..."
"... to all the upright (who belong) to (the body of) Christ Jesus ..."

Philippians 1:13
... ὥστε τοὺς δεσμούς μου φανεροὺς ἐν Χριστῷ γενέσθαι ἐν ὅλῳ τῷ πραιτωρίῳ καὶ τοῖς λοιποῖς πάσιν ...

Syntax: ἐν Χριστῷ may be considered adverbial modifying φανεροὺς 'known'.

Suggested translations:
"... so that my imprisonment has become known in the whole praetorian guard and to all the rest because of (my activity for) Christ ..."
(LB) "... because I am a Christian ..."
(CBW) "... in (the service of) Christ ..."

Philippians 1:14
... καὶ τοὺς πλείονας τῶν ἀδελφῶν ἐν κυρίῳ πεποιθότας τοῖς δεσμοῖς μου περισσοτέρως τολμᾶν ἀφόβως τὸν λόγον λαλεῖν.

Syntax: ἐν κυρίῳ may serve (1) as an adjective modifying ἀδελφῶν 'brothers', or (2) as an adverb modifying πεποιθότας 'being confident'.

Suggested translations:
For (1) "... most of the believing brothers ..."
For (2) "... made confident by the Lord ..."

Philippians 1:26
... ἵνα τὸ καύχημα ὑμῶν περισσεύῃ ἐν Χριστῷ Ἰησοῦ ἐν ἐμοὶ διὰ τῆς ἐμῆς παρουσίας πάλιν πρὸς ὑμᾶς.

Syntax: This phrase seems to be adverbial. (1) If Paul's order is chiastic, ἐν Χριστῷ Ἰησοῦ modifies περισσεύῃ 'may abound' and ἐν ἐμοί 'in me' is to be construed with καύχημα 'the boast'. (2) There is also the possibility that ἐν Χριστῷ Ἰησοῦ should be construed with the verbal idea in καύχημα 'the boast' and ἐν ἐμοὶ 'in me' with περισσεύῃ 'may abound'.

Suggested translations:

For (1) "... in order that your reason for proud boasting in me may be more than sufficient because of Christ Jesus through my coming to you again."

"... in order that your boasting in me may abound in a Christian way because of my coming to you again."

For (2) "... in order that your reason for proud boasting about Christ Jesus may be very clear in my case because of my coming to you again."

"... in order that your Christian boasting in me may be very active because of my coming to you again."

Philippians 2:1

Εἴ τις οὖν παράκλησις ἐν Χριστῷ ...

Syntax: ἐν Χριστῷ is adverbial modifying a verb like ἐστι 'is' or εὑρίσκεται 'is found' to be supplied.

Suggested translations:

"If then (there is) any encouragement in (belonging to the body of) Christ ..."

"If then Christ (is) a source of any encouragement ..."

"If then (there is) any encouragement because of (the work of) Christ ..."

(CBW) "So, if (there is) any appeal in (our union with) Christ ..."

"If then there is any encouragement (coming from faith) in Christ ..."

"If then there is any encouragement in (your communion with) Christ ..."

Philippians 2:5

τοῦτο φρονεῖτε ἐν ὑμῖν ὃ καὶ ἐν Χριστῷ Ἰησοῦ ...

Syntax: ἐν Χριστῷ Ἰησοῦ is adverbial. What it modifies depends on how one completes the ellipsis. (1) ἦν 'was' may be supplied. ... ὃ καὶ (ἦν) ἐν Χριστῷ Ἰησοῦ ... (2) a second φρονεῖτε 'think' may be understood.... ὃ καὶ (φρονεῖτε) ἐν Χριστῷ Ἰησοῦ ...

Suggested translations:

For (1) (CBW) "Keep on fostering the same disposition that Christ Jesus had ..."

(WFB) "Think just as Christ Jesus thought ..."

For (2) (BAGD) "... have the same thoughts among yourselves as you have in (your communion with) Christ Jesus ..."

Philippians 2:19
Ἐλπίζω δὲ ἐν κυρίῳ Ἰησοῦ Τιμόθεον ταχέως πέμψαι ὑμῖν ...
Syntax: ἐν κυρίῳ Ἰησοῦ may serve as an adverb (1) modifying ἐλπίζω 'I hope', or (2) πέμψαι 'to send'.
Suggested translations:
For (1) "I have hope based on the Lord Jesus ..."
For (2) "I hope with the help of the Lord Jesus ..."

Philippians 2:24
... πέποιθα δὲ ἐν κυρίῳ ὅτι καὶ αὐτὸς ταχέως ἐλεύσομαι.
Syntax: ἐν κυρίῳ serves as an adverb modifying πέποιθα 'I am confident'.
Suggested translation:
"I am trusting the Lord that I will come to you soon."

Philippians 2:29
προσδέχεσθε οὖν αὐτὸν ἐν κυρίῳ μετὰ πάσης χαρᾶς ...
Syntax: ἐν κυρίῳ may serve (1) as an adverb modifying προσδέχεσθε 'welcome', or (2) as a substantive meaning '(a person) in the Lord' in apposition with αὐτόν 'him'.
Suggested translations:
For (1) "Welcome him, then, because he is a believer ..."
For (2) "Welcome him, then, as a believer ..."
"You, then, as a believer, welcome him ..."

Philippians 3:1
Τὸ λοιπόν, ἀδελφοί μου, χαίρετε ἐν κυρίῳ.
Syntax: ἐν κυρίῳ may serve (1) as an adverb modifying χαίρετε 'rejoice', or (2) as a substantive meaning '(people) in the Lord' in apposition with the subject of χαίρετε 'rejoice'.
Suggested translations:
For (1) "Rejoice (because of what) the Lord (has done)."
"Rejoice (because of what) the Lord (is doing)."
For (2) "Rejoice as believers in the Lord."

Philippians 3:3
ἡμεῖς γάρ ἐσμεν ἡ περιτομή, οἱ πνεύματι θεοῦ λατρεύοντες καὶ καυχώμενοι ἐν Χριστῷ Ἰησοῦ καὶ οὐκ ἐν σαρκὶ πεποιθόντες ...
Syntax: ἐν Χριστῷ Ἰησοῦ is an adverbial modifier of καυχώμενοι 'glorying'.

Suggested translation:
>(NIV) "For it is we who are the circumcision, we who worship by the Spirit of God, who glory in Christ Jesus, and who put no confidence in the flesh . . ."

Philippians 3:9
. . . καὶ εὑρεθῶ ἐν αὐτῷ . . .
Syntax: ἐν αὐτῷ 'in him' may serve as an adverb modifying a participle to be supplied such as ὤν 'being' which would modify the subject of εὑρεθῶ 'I may be found'.
Suggested translation:
>". . . and I may be found (to be a person trusting) in the Lord . . ."

Philippians 3:14
. . . κατὰ σκοπὸν διώκω εἰς τὸ βραβεῖον τῆς ἄνω κλήσεως τοῦ θεοῦ ἐν Χριστῷ Ἰησοῦ.
Syntax: ἐν Χριστῷ Ἰησοῦ is adverbial indicating (1) the intermediate agent by whom God performs the action of κλήσεως 'invitation', (2) the cause for the same action, or (3) the sphere within which the calling takes place.
Suggested translations:
For (1) ". . . I press on to the goal for the prize (which is) the invitation to heaven (given me) through Christ Jesus."
For (2) ". . . (given me) because of (what) Christ Jesus (has done)."
For (3) ". . . (given me) (as one who is) in (the body of) Christ Jesus."

Philippians 4:1
Ὥστε, ἀδελφοί μου ἀγαπητοὶ καὶ ἐπιπόθητοι, χαρὰ καὶ στέφανός μου, οὕτως **στήκετε ἐν κυρίῳ**, ἀγαπητοί.
Syntax: ἐν κυρίῳ serves as an adverb modifying στήκετε 'you stand'
Suggested translation:
>". . . stand firm with (the help of the) Lord . . ."

Philippians 4:2
Εὐοδίαν παρακαλῶ καὶ Συντύχην παρακαλῶ τὸ αὐτὸ **φρονεῖν ἐν κυρίῳ**.
Syntax: ἐν κυρίῳ may serve as an adverb modifying (1) φρονεῖν 'to think', or (2) παρακαλῶ 'I urge'.
Suggested translations:
For (1) ". . . to agree with each other with the Lord's (help)."
". . . to agree with each other (because you belong to) the Lord."

For (2) "... I plead ... in (the name of) the Lord."

Philippians 4:4
Χαίρετε ἐν κυρίῳ πάντοτε ...
Syntax: ἐν κυρίῳ may serve (1) as an adverb modifying χαίρετε 'rejoice' or (2) as a substantive meaning '(people) in the Lord,' in apposition with the subject of χαίρετε 'rejoice'.
Suggested translations:
For (1) "Rejoice (because of what) the Lord (is doing) ..."
"Rejoice (because of what) the Lord (has done) ..."
For (2) "As believers rejoice ..."

Philippians 4:7
καὶ ἡ εἰρήνη τοῦ θεοῦ ἡ ὑπερέχουσα πάντα νοῦν φρουρήσει τὰς καρδίας ὑμῶν καὶ τὰ νοήματα ὑμῶν ἐν Χριστῷ Ἰησοῦ.
Syntax: ἐν Χριστῷ Ἰησοῦ may be considered (1) adverbial modifying φρουρήσει 'will guard', or (2) substantival, meaning '(people) in Christ Jesus'.
Suggested translations:
For (1) "... will guard your hearts and your thoughts because of (the power of) Christ Jesus."
"... will guard your hearts and your thoughts (by faith) in Christ Jesus."
(LB) "... (as you trust) in Christ Jesus.'
For (2) "... will guard the hearts and thoughts of you (who are members of the body of) Christ Jesus."

Philippians 4:10
Ἐχάρην δὲ ἐν κυρίῳ μεγάλως ...
Syntax: ἐν κυρίῳ may be considered a substantive meaning '(a person) in the Lord' in apposition with the subject of ἐχάρην 'I rejoiced'.
Suggested translation:
"As a believer I rejoice greatly ..."

Philippians 4:13
πάντα ἰσχύω ἐν τῷ ἐνδυναμοῦντί με.
Syntax: ἐν τῷ ἐνδυναμοῦντί με 'in the one empowering me' serves as an adverb modifying ἰσχύω 'I am able', indicating (1) the source of the strength claimed in ἰσχύω or (2) the sphere in which Paul was living.
Suggested translation:
For (1) (NIV) "I can do everything through him who gives me strength."

For (2) "I am able (to live in any circumstance since I am in felllowship) with him who strengthens me."

Philippians 4:19
ὁ δὲ θεός μου πληρώσει πᾶσαν χρείαν ὑμῶν κατὰ τὸ πλοῦτος αὐτοῦ ἐν δόξῃ ἐν Χριστῷ Ἰησοῦ.
Syntax: ἐν Χριστῷ Ἰησοῦ may be considered (1) adverbial modifying πληρώσει 'will fill', (2) adjectival modifying πλοῦτος 'riches', or (3) adjectival modifying δόξῃ 'glory'.
Suggested translations:
For (1) "And because of (what) Christ Jesus (has done), God will fill your every need according to his riches in glory."
For (2) "And according to His glorious riches (which have been provided) by Christ Jesus, God will fill your every need."
For (3) "And according to his riches in the glory which Christ Jesus has, God will fill your every need."

Philippians 4:21
Ἀσπάσασθε πάντα ἅγιον ἐν Χριστῷ Ἰησοῦ.
Syntax: ἐν Χριστῷ Ἰησοῦ may be considered (1) substantival, meaning '(people) in Christ Jesus', modified by ἅγιον 'saint', or (2) adverbial modifying ἅγιον 'saint'.
Suggested translations:
For (1) "Greet every upright Christian."
(LB) "Say 'hello' for me to all the Christians there."
For (2) "Greet everyone (who is) holy (through faith) in Christ Jesus."
". . . because of (the finished work of) Christ Jesus."

Colossians 1:2
. . . τοῖς ἐν Κολοσσαῖς ἁγίοις καὶ πιστοῖς ἀδελφοῖς ἐν Χριστῷ . . .
Syntax: ἐν Χριστῷ may be considered (1) adjectival modifying ἀδελφοῖς 'brothers', or (2) adverbial modifying ἁγίοις 'saints' and/or πιστοῖς 'faithful'.
Suggested translations:
For (1) ". . . to the holy and dependable brothers who belong to the body of Christ (who are) in Colosse . . ."
(LB) "To: The faithful Christian brothers—God's people—in the city of Colosse."
For (2) ". . . to the brothers in Colosse, holy and dependable because of (the work of) Christ (done in their lives) . . ."
". . . to the brothers in Colosse (who are) God's people and believe in Christ . . ."

Colossians 1:4
... ἀκούσαντες τὴν πίστιν ὑμῶν ἐν Χριστῷ Ἰησοῦ ...
Syntax: ἐν Χριστῷ Ἰησοῦ is (1) adverbial modifying the idea of believing in πίστιν 'faith', or (2) adjectival modifying πίστιν 'faith.'
Suggested translations:
For (1) (WFB) "... because we have heard how you believe in Christ Jesus ..."
(NEB) "... because we have heard of the faith you hold in Christ Jesus ..."
For (2) "... because we have heard of your Christian faith ..."

Colossians 1:14
... ἐν ᾧ ἔχομεν τὴν ἀπολύτρωσιν ...
Syntax: ἐν ᾧ 'in whom' serves as an adverb modifying ἔχομεν 'we have'.
Suggested translations:
"... because we are united with him we have redemption ..."
"... because we are believers we have redemption ..."

Colossians 1:16
... ὅτι ἐν αὐτῷ ἐκτίσθη τὰ πάντα ἐν τοῖς οὐρανοῖς καὶ ἐπὶ τῆς γῆς ... τὰ πάντα δι' αὐτοῦ καὶ εἰς αὐτὸν ἔκτισται ...
Syntax: ἐν αὐτῷ 'in him' serves as an adverb modifying ἐκτίσθη 'was created'.
Suggested translation:
(NIV) "For by him all things were created ..."

Colossians 1:17
... καὶ τὰ πάντα ἐν αὐτῷ συνέστηκεν ...
Syntax: ἐν αὐτῷ 'in him' serves as an adverb modifying συνέστηκεν 'stand together'.
Suggested translation:
(NIV) "... in him all things hold together ..."
"... by his (power) all things hold together ..."

Colossians 1:19
... ὅτι ἐν αὐτῷ εὐδόκησεν πᾶν τὸ πλήρωμα κατοικῆσαι ...
Syntax: ἐν αὐτῷ 'in him' is an adverb modifying κατοικῆσαι 'to dwell'.
Suggested translation:
(NIV) "For God was pleased to have all his fullness dwell in him."

Colossians 1:28
... ἵνα παραστήσωμεν πάντα ἄνθρωπον τέλειον ἐν Χριστῷ ...
Syntax: ἐν Χριστῷ may be considered (1) adverbial modifying τέλειον 'mature', or (2) substantival, meaning '(a person) in Christ'.
Suggested translations:
For (1) "... that we may present every man complete (mature) because of (the work of) Christ ..."
(LB) "... perfect because of (what) Christ (has done for each of them.)
For (2) (NEB) "... so as to present each one (of you) as a mature (member) of Christ's (body)."
"... mature in (his relationship to) Christ ..."

Colossians 2:3
... ἐν ᾧ εἰσιν πάντες οἱ θησαυροὶ τῆς σοφίας καὶ γνώσεως ἀπόκρυφοι.
Syntax: ἐν ᾧ 'in whom' serves as an adverb modifying εἰσιν ... ἀπόκρυφοι 'are hidden'.
Suggested translation:
"... in whom are hidden ..."

Colossians 2:6
Ὡς οὖν παρελάβετε τὸν Χριστὸν Ἰησοῦν τὸν κύριον, ἐν αὐτῷ περιπατεῖτε ...
Syntax: ἐν αὐτῷ 'in him' serves as an adverb modifying περιπατεῖτε 'to walk' or 'to live'.
Suggested translations:
"... live in obedience to him ..."
"... go on living in obedience to him ..."

Colossians 2:7
... ἐρριζωμένοι καὶ ἐποικοδομούμενοι ἐν αὐτῷ καὶ βεβαιούμενοι τῇ πίστει καθὼς ἐδιδάχθητε ...
Syntax: ἐν αὐτῷ 'in him' serves as an adverb modifying ἐρριζωμένοι 'rooted' and ἐποικοδομούμενοι 'being built upon'.
Suggested translations:
"... being firmly established on (rooted in) and built up on him ..."
"... having been firmly established and being built up on him ..."

Colossians 2:9
... ὅτι ἐν αὐτῷ κατοικεῖ πᾶν τὸ πλήρωμα τῆς θεότητος σωματικῶς ...
Syntax: ἐν αὐτῷ 'in him' serves as an adverb modifying κατοικεῖ 'dwells'.
Suggested translation:
> (NIV) "For in Christ all the fullness of the Deity lives in bodily form."

Colossians 2:10
... καὶ ἐστε ἐν αὐτῷ πεπληρωμένοι, ὅς ἐστιν ἡ κεφαλὴ πάσης ἀρχῆς καὶ ἐξουσίας.
Syntax: ἐν αὐτῷ 'in him' serves as an adverb modifying ἐστε ... πεπληρωμένοι 'you have been filled'.
Suggested translations:
> "... and you have been filled by Christ."
> (NIV) "... and you have been given fullness in Christ."

Colossians 2:11
ἐν ᾧ καὶ περιετμήθητε περιτομῇ ἀχειροποιήτῳ ἐν τῇ ἀπεκδύσει τοῦ σώματος τῆς σαρκός, ἐν τῇ περιτομῇ τοῦ Χριστοῦ ...
Syntax: ἐν ᾧ 'in whom' serves as an adverb modifying περιετμήθητε 'you have been circumcised'.
Suggested translation:
> (NIV) "In him you were also circumcised..."
> "(Because you were identified) with him you also have been circumcised..."

Colossians 2:12
... συνταφέντες αὐτῷ ἐν τῷ βαπτισμῷ ἐν ᾧ καὶ συνηγέρθητε διὰ τῆς πίστεως τῆς ἐνεργείας τοῦ θεοῦ τοῦ ἐγείραντος αὐτὸν ἐκ νεκρῶν ...
Syntax: ἐν ᾧ 'in whom' serves as an adverb modifying συνηγέρθητε 'you have been raised with'. The antecedent of ᾧ is Christ.
Suggested translation:
> "... having been buried with him in baptism and raised with him through your faith in the power of God, who raised him from the dead."

Colossians 3:18
Αἱ γυναῖκες, ὑποτάσσεσθε τοῖς ἀνδράσιν ὡς ἀνῆκεν ἐν κυρίῳ.
Syntax: ἐν κυρίῳ serves as an adverb modifying ἀνῆκεν 'is fitting'.
Suggested translations:
> (NIV) "... as is fitting in the Lord."

"... as Christian wives ought to do ..."

Colossians 3:20
Τὰ τέκνα, ὑπακούετε τοῖς γονεῦσιν κατὰ πάντα, τοῦτο γὰρ **εὐάρεστόν ἐστιν ἐν κυρίῳ**.
Syntax: ἐν κυρίῳ serves as an adverb modifying εὐάρεστον 'acceptable'.
Suggested translations:
(NIV) "... this pleases the Lord."
"... the Lord is pleased with this."

Colossians 4:7
Τὰ κατ' ἐμὲ πάντα γνωρίσει ὑμῖν Τυχικὸς ὁ ἀγαπητὸς ἀδελφὸς καὶ πιστὸς διάκονος καὶ **σύνδουλος ἐν κυρίῳ** ...
Syntax: ἐν κυρίῳ serves as an adjective modifying σύνδουλος 'fellow servant'.
Suggested translations:
(NIV) "... and fellow servant in the Lord ..."
"... who serves the Lord just as I do ..."

Colossians 4:17
καὶ εἴπατε Ἀρχίππῳ, **Βλέπε τὴν διακονίαν ἣν παρέλαβες ἐν κυρίῳ**, ἵνα αὐτὴν πληροῖς.
Syntax: ἐν κυρίῳ serves (1) as an adverb modifying παρέλαβες 'you have received', or (2) as a substantive, meaning 'a person in the Lord' in apposition with the subject of παρέλαβες.
Suggested translations:
For (1) (NIV) "Tell Archippus. 'See to it that you complete the work that you have received in the Lord.'"
For (2) "... Take care to carry out the work you have been given as a Christian."

1 Thessalonians 1:1
Παῦλος καὶ Σιλουανὸς καὶ Τιμόθεος **τῇ ἐκκλησίᾳ** Θεσσαλονικέων **ἐν θεῷ πατρὶ καὶ κυρίῳ Ἰησοῦ Χριστῷ**· χάρις ὑμῖν καὶ εἰρήνη.
Syntax: ἐν θεῷ πατρὶ καὶ κυρίῳ Ἰησοῦ Χριστῷ 'in God the Father and the Lord Jesus Christ' serves as an adjective modifying either (1) τῇ ἐκκλησίᾳ 'the church' or (2) Θεσσαλονικέων 'Thessalonians'.
Suggested translations:
For (1) "... to the Thessalonians' church (which belongs) to God the Father and the Lord Jesus Christ ..."
"... to the church composed of Thessalonians which is in union with God the Father and the Lord Jesus Christ ..."

For (2) "... to the church of the Thessalonians who are in union with God the Father and the Lord Jesus Christ..."
(NEB) "... to the congregation of Thessalonians who belong to God the Father and the Lord Jesus Christ..."

1 Thessalonians 2:14
ὑμεῖς γὰρ μιμηταὶ ἐγενήθητε, ἀδελφοί, τῶν ἐκκλησιῶν τοῦ θεοῦ τῶν οὐσῶν ἐν τῇ Ἰουδαίᾳ ἐν Χριστῷ Ἰησοῦ...
Syntax: ἐν Χριστῷ Ἰησοῦ may be considered (1) substantival, meaning '(people) in Christ Jesus', in apposition with ἐκκλησιῶν 'churches', or (2) adverbial modifying οὐσῶν 'being'.
Suggested translations:
For (1) "For it has turned out, brothers, that you have had the same experiences as God's churches, the Christians who are in Judea..."
For (2) "... God's churches, which exist in Judea because of (what) Christ Jesus (has done)..."

1 Thessalonians 3:8
... ὅτι νῦν ζῶμεν ἐὰν ὑμεῖς στήκετε ἐν κυρίῳ.
Syntax: ἐν κυρίῳ serves as an adverb modifying στήκετε 'you stand'.
Suggested translation:
"... if you are standing firm in (the strength of the) Lord."

1 Thessalonians 4:1
Λοιπὸν οὖν, ἀδελφοί, ἐρωτῶμεν ὑμᾶς καὶ παρακαλοῦμεν ἐν κυρίῳ Ἰησοῦ...
Syntax: ἐν κυρίῳ Ἰησοῦ serves as an adverb modifying παρακαλοῦμεν 'we urge' and ἐρωτῶμεν 'we ask'.
Suggested translations:
"... we ask you and urge you in (the name of the) Lord Jesus..."
"... because you are believers we ask you and urge you..."
"... (because of what the) Lord Jesus (has done for you) we ask you and urge you..."

1 Thessalonians 4:16
... καὶ οἱ νεκροὶ ἐν Χριστῷ ἀναστήσονται πρῶτον...
Syntax: ἐν Χριστῷ is adjectival, modifying νεκροί 'dead (people)'
Suggested translation:
"... and the Christian dead will rise first..."

1 Thessalonians 5:12
Ἐρωτῶμεν δὲ ὑμᾶς, ἀδελφοί, εἰδέναι τοὺς κοπιῶντας ἐν ὑμῖν καὶ προϊσταμένους ὑμῶν ἐν κυρίῳ καὶ νουθετοῦντας ὑμᾶς . . .
Syntax: ἐν κυρίῳ serves as an adverb modifying προϊσταμένους 'being over' and probably also νουθετοῦντας 'warning'.
Suggested translation:
> (NIV) "Now we ask you, brothers, to respect those who work hard among you, who are over you in the Lord and who admonish you."
> ". . . who are over you (under the) Lord's (direction) . . ."

1 Thessalonians 5:18
. . . ἐν παντὶ εὐχαριστεῖτε· τοῦτο γὰρ θέλημα θεοῦ ἐν Χριστῷ Ἰησοῦ εἰς ὑμᾶς.
Syntax: ἐν Χριστῷ Ἰησοῦ may be considered (1) adverbial modifying the verbal idea in θέλημα 'will', or (2) substantival, meaning '(people) in Christ Jesus' in apposition with ὑμᾶς 'you'.
Suggested translations:
For (1) ". . . for this is God's will for you (because you belong to) Christ Jesus."
> ". . . (because you are united) with Christ Jesus."
> ". . . (because of the work done) by Christ Jesus."
> ". . . because of Christ Jesus."

For (2) ". . . for this is God's will for you Christians."

2 Thessalonians 1:12
. . . ὅπως ἐνδοξασθῇ τὸ ὄνομα τοῦ κυρίου ἡμῶν Ἰησοῦ ἐν ὑμῖν, καὶ ὑμεῖς ἐν αὐτῷ, κατὰ τὴν χάριν τοῦ θεοῦ ἡμῶν καὶ κυρίου Ἰησοῦ Χριστοῦ.
Syntax: ἐν αὐτῷ 'in him' may be considered an adverb modifying ἐνδοξασθῇ 'you may be glorified' to be supplied with ὑμεῖς 'you'.
Suggested translations:
> "(We pray) that the name of our Jesus may be glorified among you and (that) you (may) be glorified in him . . ."
> ". . . be glorified by him . . ."
> ". . . be glorified (as a part of) his (body) . . ."
> ". . . be glorified in (association with) him . . ."

2 Thessalonians 3:4
πεποίθαμεν δὲ ἐν κυρίῳ ἐφ' ὑμᾶς, ὅτι ἃ παραγγέλλομεν καὶ ποιεῖτε καὶ ποιήσετε.
Syntax: ἐν κυρίῳ serves as an adverb to modify πεποίθαμεν 'we are confident'.

Suggested translation:
> (NIV) "We have confidence in the Lord that you are doing and will continue to do the things we command."

2 Thessalonians 3:12
... τοῖς δὲ τοιούτοις παραγγέλλομεν καὶ παρακαλοῦμεν ἐν κυρίῳ Ἰησοῦ Χριστῷ ...

Syntax: ἐν κυρίῳ Ἰησοῦ Χριστῷ is adverbial modifying παραγγέλλομεν 'charge' and παρακαλοῦμεν 'exhort'.

Suggested translations:
> (CBW) "Now on (the authority of) the Lord Jesus Christ we charge and exhort such persons..."
> (LB) "In (the name of) the Lord Jesus Christ we appeal to such people—we command them—..."

1 Timothy 1:14
... ὑπερεπλεόνασεν δὲ ἡ χάρις τοῦ κυρίου ἡμῶν μετὰ πίστεως καὶ ἀγάπης τῆς ἐν Χριστῷ Ἰησοῦ.

Syntax: ἐν Χριστῷ Ἰησοῦ is an adjective in restrictive attributive position modifying ἀγάπης 'love' and quite possibly also πίστεως 'faith'.

Suggested translations:
> (NASB) "... and the grace of our Lord was more than abundant, with the faith and love (which are found) in Christ Jesus."
> "... and the grace of our Lord along with the faithfulness and love (which) Christ Jesus (has shown to me) proved very abundant."

1 Timothy 3:13
... οἱ γὰρ καλῶς διακονήσαντες βαθμὸν ἑαυτοῖς καλὸν περιποιοῦνται καὶ πολλὴν παρρησίαν ἐν πίστει τῇ ἐν Χριστῷ Ἰησοῦ.

Syntax: ἐν Χριστῷ Ἰησοῦ serves as an adjective in restrictive attributive position, modifying πίστει 'faith'.

Suggested translations:
> (WFB) "When they have served well, they get a good standing and can talk very confidently of their faith in Christ Jesus."
> (NEB) "For deacons with a good record of service may claim a high standing and the right to speak openly on matters of the Christian faith."

2 Timothy 1:1
Παῦλος ἀπόστολος Χριστοῦ Ἰησοῦ διὰ θελήματος θεοῦ κατ' ἐπαγγελίαν ζωῆς τῆς ἐν Χριστῷ Ἰησοῦ ...
Syntax: ἐν Χριστῷ Ἰησοῦ serves as an adjective in restrictive attributive position modifying ζωῆς 'life'.
Suggested translations:
"... according to the promise of life (which has its source (origin)) in Christ Jesus ..."
"... according to the promise of the Christian life ..."
"... according to the promise of the life (which is possible) because of (what) Christ Jesus (has done) ..."

2 Timothy 1:9
... ἀλλὰ κατὰ ἰδίαν πρόθεσιν καὶ χάριν, τὴν δοθεῖσαν ἡμῖν ἐν Χριστῷ Ἰησοῦ πρὸ χρόνων αἰωνίων ...
Syntax: ἐν Χριστῷ Ἰησοῦ is adverbial modifying δοθεῖσαν 'given'.
Suggested translations:
"... but according to His own purpose and favor which were given to us in Christ Jesus (when we were made members of His body) ..."
"... which were given to us (because we are) in (the body of) Christ Jesus ..."

2 Timothy 1:13
ὑποτύπωσιν ἔχε ὑγιαινόντων λόγων ὧν παρ' ἐμοῦ ἤκουσας ἐν πίστει καὶ ἀγάπῃ τῇ ἐν Χριστῷ Ἰησοῦ ...
Syntax: ἐν Χριστῷ Ἰησοῦ serves as an adjective in restrictive attributive position modifying ἀγάπῃ 'love' and quite possibly πίστει 'faithfulness'.
Suggested translations:
"Keep hold of the standard of correct statements which you have heard from me (spoken) with the faithfulness and love (which) Christ Jesus (has shown to me) ..."
"... with the faithfulness and love (which are provided) by Christ Jesus ..."

2 Timothy 2:1
Σὺ οὖν, τέκνον μου, ἐνδυναμοῦ ἐν τῇ χάριτι τῇ ἐν Χριστῷ Ἰησοῦ ...
Syntax: ἐν Χριστῷ Ἰησοῦ serves as an adjective in restrictive attributive position modifying χάριτι 'grace'.
Suggested translations:
"You, therefore, my son, become strong in the favor (which is provided) by Christ Jesus ..."
"... the favor (which has its source) in Christ Jesus ..."

2 Timothy 2:10
... ἵνα καὶ αὐτοὶ σωτηρίας τύχωσιν τῆς ἐν Χριστῷ Ἰησοῦ μετὰ δόξης αἰωνίου.
Syntax: ἐν Χριστῷ Ἰησοῦ serves as an adjective in restrictive attributive position, modifying σωτηρίας 'salvation'.
Suggested translations:
"... in order that they themselves also may obtain the salvation (which has been provided) by Christ Jesus (and) with (it) everlasting glory."
"... in order that they themselves also may secure with everlasting glory the salvation which (is given by faith) in Christ Jesus."
"... the salvation which (has) Christ Jesus (as its source)."

2 Timothy 3:12
καὶ πάντες δὲ οἱ θέλοντες εὐσεβῶς ζῆν ἐν Χριστῷ Ἰησοῦ διωχθήσονται.
Syntax: ἐν Χριστῷ Ἰησοῦ may be considered adverbial modifying (1) ζῆν 'to live', or (2) εὐσεβῶς 'godly', or (3) διωχθήσονται 'will be persecuted', or (4) substantival as a predicate nominative with διωχθήσονται 'will be persecuted'.
Suggested translations:
For (1) "And indeed all who want to live by (the power of) Christ Jesus in a godly way will be persecuted."
For (2) "and indeed all who want to live godly lives (in harmony with their faith) in Christ Jesus will be persecuted."
For (3) "And indeed all who want to live godly lives will be persecuted because they are Christians."
For (4) "And indeed all who want to live godly lives will be persecuted as Christians."

2 Timothy 3:15
... καὶ ὅτι ἀπὸ βρέφους τὰ ἱερὰ γράμματα οἶδας, τὰ δυνάμενά σε σοφίσαι εἰς σωτηρίαν διὰ πίστεως τῆς ἐν Χριστῷ Ἰησοῦ.
Syntax: ἐν Χριστῷ Ἰησοῦ serves as an adjective in restrictive attributive position modifying πίστεως 'faith'.
Suggested translations:
"... that since childhood you have known the holy Scriptures which can lead you (by their instruction) into (the) salvation (which is given) by believing in Christ Jesus."
"... the salvation (which is available) through faith (which is fixed) in Christ Jesus."

Philemon 8
Διό πολλὴν ἐν Χριστῷ παρρησίαν ἔχων ἐπιτάσσειν σοι τὸ ἀνῆκον . . .

Syntax: ἐν Χριστῷ may be considered (1) adverbial modifying ἔχων 'having', (2) adjectival modifying παρρησίαν 'confidence', (3) adverbial modifying πολλήν 'much', or (4) substantival, meaning '(a person) in Christ', in apposition with the subject of παρακαλῶ 'I appeal' in vs. 9.

Suggested translations:
For (1) "Therefore, although I have (because of the authority given me) by Christ strong confidence to command you (to do) your duty . . ."
For (2) "Therefore, although I have strong confidence (based) on (the authority of) Christ to command you (to do) your duty . . ."
For (3) "Therefore, although my confidence is strong (because of the authority given me) by Christ . . ."
For (4) "Therefore, although as a Christian I have strong confidence to command you . . ."

Philemon 16
. . . οὐκέτι ὡς δοῦλον ἀλλὰ ὑπὲρ δοῦλον, ἀδελφὸν ἀγαπητόν, μάλιστα ἐμοί, πόσῳ δὲ μᾶλλον σοὶ καὶ ἐν σαρκὶ καὶ ἐν κυρίῳ.

Syntax: ἐν κυρίῳ may be considered (1) an adverb modifying ἀγαπητόν 'loved', or (2) an adjective modifying ἀδελφόν 'brother'.

Suggested translations:
For (1) ". . . a brother loved because he is a believer . . ."
For (2) ". . . a Christian brother who is loved . . ."

Philemon 20a
ναί, ἀδελφέ, ἐγώ σου ὀναίμην ἐν κυρίῳ . . .

Syntax: ἐν κυρίῳ serves as an adverb modifying ὀναίμην 'may I benefit'.

Suggested translations:
(BAGD) ". . . let me have some benefit from you in the Lord . . ."
(NIV) ". . . that I may have some benefit from you in the Lord . . ."

Philemon 20b
ἀνάπαυσόν μου τὰ σπλάγχνα ἐν Χριστῷ.

Syntax: ἐν Χριστῷ may be considered (1) adverbial modifying ἀνάπαυσόν 'refresh', or (2) substantival, meaning '(a person)

in Christ' in apposition with the subject of ἀνάπαυσόν 'refresh'.
Suggested translations:
For (1) "... refresh my heart because of Christ."
"... refresh my heart because of (what) Christ (has done)."
For (2) "... as a Christian refresh my heart."

Philemon 23
Ἀσπάζεταί σε Ἐπαφρᾶς ὁ συναιχμάλωτός μου ἐν Χριστῷ Ἰησοῦ ...
Syntax: ἐν Χριστῷ Ἰησοῦ may be considered (1) substantival, meaning '(a person) in Christ Jesus', or (2) adverbial, modifying ἀσπάζεταί 'greets'.
Suggested translations:
For (1) "Epaphras, my Christian fellow captive, greets you."
"Epaphras, my fellow captive in (the cause of) Christ, greets you."
For (2) "Epaphras, my fellow captive, sends you Christian greetings."

1 Peter 3:16
... ἵνα ἐν ᾧ καταλαλεῖσθε καταισχυνθῶσιν οἱ ἐπηρεάζοντες ὑμῶν τὴν ἀγαθὴν ἐν Χριστῷ ἀναστροφήν.
Syntax: ἐν Χριστῷ serves as an adjective in ascriptive attributive position modifying ἀναστροφήν 'conduct'.
Suggested translations:
"... your good Christian conduct."
"... your good behavior as Christians."

1 Peter 5:10
Ὁ δὲ θεὸς πάσης χάριτος, ὁ καλέσας ὑμᾶς εἰς τὴν αἰώνιον αὐτοῦ δόξαν ἐν Χριστῷ ...
Syntax: ἐν Χριστῷ serves (1) as an adverb modifying καλέσας 'has called', or (2) as an adjective modifying δόξαν 'glory'.
Suggested translations:
For (1) "... who has invited you into his everlasting glory (because of the work done) by Christ ..."
"... who has called you into his eternal glory because you belong to Christ ..."
For (2) "... who has called you into the eternal glory which he has in Christ Jesus ..."

1 Peter 5:14
εἰρήνη ὑμῖν πᾶσιν τοῖς ἐν Χριστῷ.
Syntax: ἐν Χριστῷ is substantival, meaning '(people) in Christ' in apposition with ὑμῖν 'you'.
Suggested translations:
"May all of you Christians have peace."
"Peace be to all of you who (belong) to (the body of) Christ."

1 John 2:8
πάλιν ἐντολὴν καινὴν γράφω ὑμῖν **ὅ ἐστιν αληθὲς ἐν αὐτῷ καὶ ἐν ὑμῖν**, ὅτι ἡ σκοτία παράγεται καὶ τὸ φῶς τὸ ἀληθινὸν ἤδη φαίνει.
Syntax: ἐν αὐτῷ 'in him' serves as an adverb modifying αληθές 'true'.
Suggested translations:
(NIV) ". . . its truth is seen in him and in you . . ."
". . . the truth of its (necessity) . . ."
". . . the truth of its (operating principle) . . ."
". . . the truth of its (permanence) . . ."
". . . the truth of its (effective essence) . . ."
". . . the truth of its (effective operation) . . ."
". . . the truth of its (essential validity) . . ."
Expanded paraphrase:
"It is a command the obedience to which has proved true in the sacrifice Christ made for us, and is proving true in your love for each other. It stands in contrast to the darkness, which passes away, and in harmony with the true light which is already shining."

1 John 2:24
ἐὰν ἐν ὑμῖν μείνῃ ὃ ἀπ' ἀρχῆς ἠκούσατε, καὶ **ὑμεῖς ἐν τῷ υἱῷ καὶ ἐν τῷ πατρὶ μενεῖτε.**
Syntax: ἐν τῷ υἱῷ 'in the Son' serves as an adverb modifying μενεῖτε 'will remain'.
Suggested translations:
". . . you will continue (to be in fellowship) with the Son and with the Father."
(TEV) ". . . you will always live in union with the Son and the Father."

1 John 2:27
. . . καὶ καθὼς ἐδίδαξεν ὑμᾶς, **μένετε ἐν αὐτῷ**.
Syntax: ἐν αὐτῷ 'in him' serves as an adverb modifying μένετε 'you remain'.

Suggested translations:
>(NIV) "... remain in him."
>"... maintain (your fellowship) with him."

1 John 2:28
Καὶ νῦν, τεκνία, **μένετε ἐν αὐτῷ**, ἵνα ἐὰν φανερωθῇ σχῶμεν παρρησίαν καὶ μὴ αἰσχυνθῶμεν ἀπ' αὐτοῦ ἐν τῇ παρουσίᾳ αὐτοῦ.
Syntax: ἐν αὐτῷ 'in him' serves as an adverb modifying μένετε 'remain'.
Suggested translations:
>(NIV) "... continue in him ..."
>"... maintain (your fellowship) with him ..."

1 John 3:5
... καὶ ἁμαρτία ἐν αὐτῷ οὐκ ἔστιν.
Syntax: ἐν αὐτῷ 'in him' serves as an adverb modifying ἔστιν 'is'.
Suggested translations:
>(NIV) "And in him is no sin."
>"And sin does not exist in him."

1 John 3:6
πᾶς ὁ ἐν αὐτῷ μένων οὐχ ἁμαρτάνει ...
Syntax: ἐν αὐτῷ 'in him' serves as an adverb modifying μένων 'remaining'.
Suggested translations:
>(NIV) "No one who lives in him keeps on sinning ..."
>"No one who maintains his fellowship with him keeps on sinning ..."

1 John 5:20
... καὶ ἐσμὲν ἐν ἀληθινῷ, ἐν τῷ υἱῷ αὐτοῦ Ἰησοῦ Χριστῷ.
Syntax: Since αὐτοῦ 'his' following υἱῷ 'Son' seems to have τῷ ἀληθινῷ 'the true one' as its antecedent, τῷ ἀληθινῷ and τῷ υἱῷ cannot refer to the same person. Therefore ἀληθινῷ points to God the Father. Both prepositional phrases serve as adverbs modifying ἐσμέν 'we are'.
Suggested translations:
>"... and we are in fellowship (or union) with the true (God), even in fellowship with his Son Jesus Christ."
>"... and we belong to the true (God, even) to his Son Jesus Christ."

Revelation 14:13
... Μακάριοι οἱ νεκροὶ οἱ ἐν κυρίῳ ἀποθνῄσκοντες ἀπ' ἄρτι.
Syntax: ἐν κυρίῳ serves as an adverb modifying ἀποθνῄσκοντες 'dying'.
Suggested translation:
    (NIV) "... Blessed are the dead who die in the Lord from now on."
    "... Blessed are those who die as Christians ..."

INDEX OF SUGGESTED TRANSLATIONS

A

a believer   Rom. 16:22; Eph. 6:21; Phil. 2:29; 4:10; Philem. 16
about Christ Jesus   Phil. 1:26
a Christian   Philem. 16
a Christian prisoner   Eph. 4:1
among Christians   1 Cor 4:15; Gal. 5:6
a person trusting in the Lord   Phil. 3:9
a prisoner bound by the Lord   Eph. 4:1
a prisoner bound for the Lord   Eph. 4:1
as a believer   Eph. 4:17
as a believer should   Rom. 16:22
as a Christian   Rom. 9:1; 14:14; 15:17; 1 Cor. 15:31; 2 Cor. 12:19; Col. 4:17; Philem. 8, 20
as a man in the body of Christ   Rom. 9:1
as a sister believing in the Lord   Rom. 16:2
as believers   Eph. 4:21; 5:8
as believers in him   1 Cor. 1:5
as believers in the Lord   Rom. 16:2; Eph. 6:1
as captives of Christ   2 Cor. 2:14
as Christians   Rom. 16:3, 9; 2 Cor. 2:17; 12:19; Gal. 2:4; 2 Tim. 3:12; 1 Pet. 3:16; Rev 14:13
as it was demonstrated in what Christ Jesus our Lord did for us   Rom. 8:39
as members of the body of Christ   Eph. 3:12
as one who belongs to the Lord   1 Cor. 1:31
as one who is in the Lord Jesus   Rom. 14:14
as part of his body   2 Thess. 1:12
as part of the body of Christ   Eph. 1:4
as people belonging to the Lord   Rom. 16:8
as people who are in his body   2 Cor 13:4
as people who believe in the Lord   1 Cor 9:1
as people who belong to the Lord   1 Cor. 16:19
as the people of the Lord   1 Cor. 16:19
as the result of a miracle performed by Jesus   Acts 4:10
as trophies belonging to Christ   2 Cor. 2:14
as you trust in Christ Jesus   Phil. 4:7

B

based on the authority of Christ Philem. 8
based on the Lord Phil. 2:19
be strengthened by the Lord Eph. 6:10
because he is a believer Rom. 16:8
because I am a Christian Phil. 1:13
because of Christ Eph. 3:21; 4:32; Phil. 1:1, 26; 1 Thess. 5:18; Philem. 20
because of him Eph. 1:4; 3:12
because of it (i.e. Jesus' name) Acts 4:10
because of Jesus Acts 4:10
because of my activity for Christ Phil. 1:13
because of our faith in Christ Eph. 1:3
because of the authority given me by Christ Philem. 8
because of the finished work of Christ Jesus Eph. 2:6; Phil. 4:21
because of the Messiah 1 Cor. 15:22
because of the power of Christ Jesus Phil. 4:7
because of the victory which Christ has won 2 Cor. 2:14
because of the work done by Christ Rom. 12:5; 1 Cor. 4:15; Gal. 2:17; 1 Pet. 5:10
because of the work done by Christ Jesus 1 Cor. 1:4; Gal. 3:14; 1 Thess. 5:18
because of the work of Christ Phil. 2:1; Col. 1:28
because of the work of Christ done in their lives Col. 1:2
because of the work of Christ Jesus Eph. 3:6
because of what Christ has done 2 Cor. 5:21; Eph. 3:12; Philem. 20
because of what Christ Jesus has done Rom. 6:11; 8:2; Gal. 2:4; Phil. 3:14; 4:19; 1 Thess. 2:14; 2 Tim. 1:1
because of what Christ Jesus has done for each of them Col. 1:28
because of what Christ Jesus our Lord has done Rom. 6:23
because of what the Lord has done 1 Cor. 1:31; 4:17; Phil. 3:1; 4:4; 1 Thess. 4:1
because of what the Lord is doing Phil. 3:1; 4:4
because of whom we have redemption Eph. 1:7
because they are Christians 2 Tim. 3:12
because we are a part of the body of his Beloved Eph. 1:6
because we are believers Col. 1:14
because we are in the body of Christ Jesus 2 Tim. 1:9
because we are united with Christ Rom. 12:5; Gal. 2:4
because we are united with him Col. 1:14
because we have placed our faith in Christ Jesus Gal. 2:4
because you are believers Eph. 5:8; 6:1; 1 Thess. 4:1
because you are identified with Christ Jesus Rom. 6:11
because you are in Christ Jesus Rom. 6:11
because you are united with Christ Jesus 1 Thess. 5:18
because you belong to Christ Eph. 4:32; 1 Pet. 5:10
because you belong to Christ Jesus 1 Thess. 5:18
because you belong to the body of Christ Jesus 1 Cor. 1:4

INDEX OF SUGGESTED TRANSLATIONS 57

because you belong to the Lord
  Phil. 4:2
because you have been united in
  Christ Gal. 3:28
because you were identified with
  him Col. 2:11
believer in the Lord 1 Cor.
  4:17; 7:39
believers Phil. 3:1; 4:4
believing Eph. 6:21; Phil. 1:14
by becoming a part of his body
  2 Cor. 5:21
by being united with Christ
  Jesus 1 Cor. 1:2
by believing in Christ 2 Cor.
  3:14
by Christ (for ἐν αὐτῷ) Col.
  2:10
by Christ Jesus Eph. 2:10; 3:21
by citing the example of Jesus'
  resurrection Acts 4:2
by faith in Christ 2 Cor. 3:14;
  Gal. 2:17
by faith in Christ Jesus Rom.
  8:2; 1 Cor. 1:2; 1:30; Gal.
  3:14; Eph. 2:6; 2:13; 3:6;
  Phil. 4:7
by him 1 Cor. 1:5; 2 Cor. 1:19;
  Eph. 4:21; Col. 1:16;
  2 Thess. 1:12
by his power Col. 1:17
by making us members of the
  body of Christ Eph. 1:3
by the Lord Phil. 1:14
by the Lord Jesus Rom. 14:14
by the power of Christ Jesus
  Rom. 8:2; 1 Cor. 1:2; 1:4;
  4:15; Eph. 2:10; 2 Tim. 3:12
by the strength of the Lord
  1 Cor. 9:1
by the work of the Lord Eph.
  2:21
by what Christ Jesus has done
  for us Eph. 2:7
by whom Eph. 2:21, 22
by working through Christ
  2 Cor. 5:19

by your union with the Lord
  Eph. 6:10

C

called by the Lord 1 Cor. 7:22
Christian Rom. 16:3, 9, 10;
  1 Cor. 4:15, 17; 2 Cor. 5:17;
  12:2; Gal. 1:22; Phil. 1:26;
  4:21; Col. 1:2, 4; 3:18;
  1 Thess. 4:16; 1 Tim. 3:13;
  2 Tim. 1:1; Philem. 20, 23; 1
  Pet. 3:16
Christians Rom. 8:1; 16:7, 9;
  1 Cor. 1:2; 3:1; 4:10; 15:18,
  19; 16:24; Gal. 2:17; Eph.
  1:1; Phil. 1:1; 4:21; 1 Thess.
  2:14; 5:18; 2 Tim. 3:12; 1
  Pet. 3:16; 5:14
Christ is my witness Rom. 9:1
Christ Jesus is the source of my
  boasting about the work
  which I have done for God
  Rom. 15:17
coming from faith in Christ
  Phil. 2:1

F

fellow servant in the Lord Col.
  4:7
fellowship with him 1 John
  2:27; 3:6

G

glory in Christ Jesus Phil. 3:3

H

healed by Jesus Acts 4:10

I

if Christ is a source of any
  encouragement Phil. 2:1
in a Christian manner Rom.
  16:3, 9
in a Christian way Rom. 16:8;
  Phil. 1:26

in associaton with him 2 Thess. 1:12
in belonging to the body of Christ Phil. 2:1
in Christ Rom. 15:17; 1 Cor. 4:17; 15:19; 2 Cor. 12:19; Eph. 1:3, 12; Col. 1:2
in Christ (for ἐν αὐτῷ) Col. 2:9, 10
in Christ Jesus Gal. 3:26; Eph. 1:1; Col. 1:4; 1 Tim. 3:13; 2 Tim. 1:9; 3:15; 1 Pet. 5:10
in Christ Jesus when we were made members of His body 2 Tim. 1:9
in dependence on the Lord Eph. 6:10
in fellowship with him Phil. 4:13
in fellowship with the Son 1 John 2:24; 5:20
in harmony with their faith in Christ Jesus 2 Tim. 3:12
in him Eph. 1:11, 13; 2:22; 4:21; Col. 1:17, 19; 2:11; 2 Thess. 1:12; 1 John 2:8, 27, 28;3:5, 6, 24
in himself Eph 2:15, 16
in his integrity 2 Cor. 1:19, 20
in his relationship to Christ Col. 1:28
in obedience to him Col. 2:6
in our identification with him 2 Cor 13:4
in our relationship to Christ Jesus Gal. 5:6
in our union with Christ Phil. 2:1
in the body of Christ Jesus Rom. 8:1; Gal. 5:6; Phil. 3:14
in the cause of Christ Rom. 16:3, 9; Philem. 23
in the Christian church 1 Cor. 4:15
in the Christian life 1 Cor. 4:15
in their Christian lives 1 Cor. 3:1
in the Lord Gal. 5:10; Eph. 6:21; Col. 3:18; 4:17; 1 Thess. 5:12; 2 Thess. 3:4; Philem 20; Rev. 14:13
in the Lord Jesus Eph. 1:15
in the Lord's strength 1 Cor. 15:58
in the Messiah Eph. 1:12
in the name of the Lord Eph. 4:1; Phil. 4:2
in the name of the Lord Jesus 1 Thess. 4:1
in the name of the Lord Jesus Christ 2 Thess. 3:12
in the person of Christ 2 Cor. 5:19
in the physical body of Christ Eph. 1:20
in the service of Christ Phil. 1:13
in the service of the Lord Rom. 16:12, 22
in the strength of the Lord 1 Thess. 3:8
in the work accomplished among you by Christ Jesus our Lord 1 Cor. 15:31
in the work done by Christ Jesus Rom. 15:17; Eph. 3:11
in the work of Christ Rom. 16:9
in the work of Christ Jesus Rom. 16:3; 1 Cor. 4:17
in union with Christ 1 Cor. 15:18
in union with the Son 1 John 2:24
in whom Eph. 1:11; Col. 2:3
in your Christian lives 1 Cor. 4:10
in your communion with Christ Jesus Phil. 2:1, 5

J

just as Christ Jesus thought Phil. 2:5

INDEX OF SUGGESTED TRANSLATIONS

L

life in Christ 1 Cor. 4:17

M

make Christ the supreme ruler Eph. 1:10a
may the church and Christ Jesus be sources of glory Eph. 3:21
member of Christ's body Col. 1:28
member of the body of Christ 2 Cor. 5:17
members of the body of Christ Rom. 16:7
members of the body of Christ Jesus 1 Cor. 1:4, 30; Eph. 2:6, 7, 10, 13; Phil. 4:7

O

of Christ Jesus Eph. 2:7
on him Col. 2:7
on the authority of the Lord Jesus Christ 2 Thess. 3:12
opened by the Lord 2 Cor. 2:12
operating with the power of Christ Jesus Rom. 8:2

S

since he was in Christ Jesus Rom. 8:2
since we are members of the body of Christ Jesus Eph. 2:6
since you have become members of the body of Christ Jesus Eph. 2:13
so Christ Jesus is the source of my boasting Rom. 15:17

T

that came by Christ Jesus Rom. 3:24
the church and Christ Jesus will be sources of glory for him Eph. 3:21
the Lord is pleased with this Col. 3:20
the same disposition that Christ Jesus had Phil. 2:5
the truth that is in Jesus Eph. 4:21
this pleases the Lord Col. 3:20
through Christ 2 Cor. 5:19; Eph. 4:32
through Christ Jesus Phil. 3:14
through Christ Jesus our Lord Eph. 3:11
through faith in Christ Jesus Phil. 4:21
through faith in Christ Jesus our Lord Rom. 6:23
through him (i.e. Christ) Eph. 1:9; Phil. 4:13
through his beloved Son Eph. 1:6
through union with Christ Rom. 12:5
through your union with Christ Jesus Eph. 2:13
trusting the Lord Phil. 2:24
truth exists in Jesus Eph. 4:21

U

under the authority of Christ Eph. 1:10
under the Lord's direction 1 Thess. 5:12
united in Christ Jesus Phil. 1:1
united with Christ 2 Cor. 5:17
united with Christ Jesus 1 Cor. 1:30

W

was working through Christ 2 Cor. 5:19
when you were made members of the body of Christ Jesus 1 Cor. 1:4

which are found in Christ Jesus 1 Tim. 1:14
which are provided by Christ Jesus 2 Tim. 1:13
which belongs to the Lord Jesus Christ 1 Thess. 1:1
which Christ Jesus has Phil. 4:19
which Christ Jesus has shown to me 1 Tim. 1:14; 2 Tim. 1:13
which exists because of what Christ Jesus has done Rom. 8:2
which has been accomplished by Christ Jesus Rom. 3:24
which has been provided by Christ Jesus Rom. 3:24; 6:23; 2 Tim. 2:10
which has Christ Jesus as its source 2 Tim. 2:10
which has its source (origin) in Christ Jesus Rom. 8:2; 2 Tim. 1:1; 2:1
which have been provided by Christ Jesus Phil. 4:19
which is provided by Christ Jesus 2 Tim. 2:1
which is a part of the privilege of being in Christ Jesus Rom. 3:24
which is a part of the privilege of one belonging to the body of Christ Jesus Rom. 8:2
which is available through faith in Christ Jesus Rom. 3:24; 6:23; 2 Tim. 3:15
which is fixed in Christ Jesus 2 Tim. 3:15
which is given by faith in Christ Jesus 2 Tim. 2:10
which is in Christ Jesus Rom. 3:24
which is in union with with the Lord Jesus Christ 1 Thess. 1:1
which operates through Christ Jesus our Lord Rom. 8:39
which is possible because of what Christ Jesus has done 2 Tim. 1:1
which would be brought about by the power of Jesus Acts 4:2
who are believers Rom. 16:11
who are Christians Rom. 16:11
who are members of the body of Christ Jesus 1 Cor. 1:4
who are members of the body of the Beloved Eph. 1:6
who believe in Christ Jesus Rom. 8:1
who belong to the body of Christ Col. 1:2; 1 Pet. 5:14
who belong to the body of Christ Jesus Eph. 1:1; Phil. 1:1
who is in Christ Jesus Rom. 6:11
who serves the Lord just as I do Col. 4:7
who was a member of the body of Christ 2 Cor. 12:2
with Christ as my witness Rom. 9:1
with Christ as our witness 2 Cor. 2:17; 12:19
with him Col. 2:12; 1 John 2:27
with his authority 2 Cor. 1:19, 20
with the help of the Lord Phil. 2:19; 4:1
with the Lord as my witness Eph. 4:17
with the Lord's blessing 1 Cor. 15:58
with the Lord's help Phil. 4:2
with the power of Christ 2 Cor. 2:17; 12:19
with the strength of the Lord Rom. 16:12
within the mystical body of Christ Jesus Eph. 3:6

www.ingramcontent.com/pod-product-compliance
Lightning Source LLC
Chambersburg PA
CBHW071823230426
43670CB00013B/2554